WITHOUT RESERVATION

MARNIE CUSHING

Names have been changed to preserve the identities of people outside my family.
All scripture is written in the English Standard Version (ESV).

Canva cover design by Jade Kiyak

DEDICATION

To my daughter, Jade.

*I thank God for your life and His grace
in allowing me to be your Momma.*

INTRODUCTION

This is my personal story. Everyone comes from different backgrounds; we travel different roads and end up miles away from where we started. It's hard not to judge others we see on the same path, but we are all individuals and make our own choices. We see things from unique perspectives. We live the only way we can: one day at a time, one choice at a time, and suffer the consequences. These are what I like to call the semicolon[1] moments of our lives -- pauses where we make a choice to stop and choose. Sometimes the pauses are more profound than what comes before or after that moment. They are gifts; a time to regroup and look at things differently. My story is by no means the standard for others who have gone through similar situations.

Unfortunately, it's too easy for those on the outside to spout theories and condescension -- to say, "If I were in that situation, I would or wouldn't do" whatever they think they see.　But the truth is, unless you've been in a specific situation, you don't know what you would do. We hope we make the right choice, but life is full of mistakes. It's what you do with the choices that count. This book is intended to be a glimpse into how I reacted in the face of some really hard decisions: the good, the bad, and the ugly. Philippians 1:6 says "And I am sure of this, that he who began a good work in you will bring it to completion at the day of Jesus Christ." God has made my life good in spite of the choices I've

---

[1] Semicolon: "A mark of punctuation (;) used to connect independent clauses and show a closer relationship than a period does.

made, and I strive to follow His will daily, knowing He has a purpose and calling I must answer.

I've made a notation that the names in this book have been changed to preserve the identities of others. Although I am willing to be honest about my past and what happened to me, I do not have the right to share other people's stories without their permission. If you are in my story, you'll know who you are. Having said that, please understand that I harbor no ill will toward any of you now, though as I go through the timeline, I may come across as angry, hurt, or defensive based on the circumstances and how I felt at the time. Realize that this account is based solely on my perception of events. A great deal of time has passed, but my desire is to be as honest as my memory allows.

If just one person can find comfort by reading this book, I will count it a success. Over the years, I have shared my testimony with many and find that God has given me this life so that I may shine His light to those living in their own personal darkness. May you find peace.

--Marnie

TABLE OF CONTENTS

PART 1;   CHOOSING THE WAY

"Enter by the narrow gate. For the gate is wide and the way is easy that leads to destruction, and those who enter by it are many. For the gate is narrow and the way is hard that leads to life, and those who find it are few."

Matthew 7:13-14

CHAPTER 1

"When we get back home, Marnie needs to go on a diet," Mama said, leaning toward Daddy while my brother and I swam at a hotel pool somewhere in the northeastern United States. It was the summer following my senior year of high school, and as part of my graduation present, my parents allowed me to choose where we would take our summer vacation.

Each year my father took a single, two-week vacation in July or August. My mother wouldn't fly, so we spent most summers traveling thousands of miles, on the backroads, seeing the country from the windows of our small car. We sang songs, played games, and watched the scenery flash by. That summer I asked to go to Nova Scotia. Thinking back, I don't remember why I wanted to go to that part of the continent, but I was intent on acquiring as many states in one trip as possible. The idea of venturing into Canada and experiencing the northeast coast intrigued me.

I have fond memories of that drive. At one point we stopped to get gas just shy of the ferry boarding in Maine before we crossed the bay into Canada. I can remember my father popping the trunk of our car to get out windbreakers because we knew the temperature would be cooler on the water. The owner of the station mentioned to one of his regular customers about how hot it was that day, "It gets much higher than 70 degrees and I can't stand it." We looked at him with our mouths agape. I think my daddy responded with something like, "Are you kidding me? It was 1140 in Texas three days ago when we left on our trip; this is cool weather to us!" The station owner was in shock. He couldn't understand how we could live in that heat.

We took one huge loop from Texas, east, up the Atlantic coast, across to Nova Scotia, PEI, and back into Ontario. I had one of the best meals of my life on that trip. We ate in a small dive, down a back alley, on Prince Edward Island (PEI), called the Off Broadway Cafe. The food was amazing; I still dream about those lobster stuffed mushrooms. We saw Niagara Falls from the Canadian side and then headed south back to Texas. I always loved traveling with my family. We made great memories and had lots of good times together, but this trip was difficult for me. Every moment was tainted by the heavy secret I carried. My mama's comment about my change in weight was a glimpse into the future.

I didn't hear her words until a few months later when my life changed forever.

A Brief History

I am a preacher's kid. My father served as a song leader, worship leader, youth minister, senior adult minister, pulpit minister, associate minister, and any other role you might think of, in multiple churches. I was in church every time the doors opened. We were the first ones to show up and the last ones to leave. When we started school, Daddy would pick up my younger brother and me from the private Christian school we attended and let us hang out in the church office until Mama got off work. My brother and I would run the buildings. To this day, I can enter a church building and figure out where everything is...restrooms, fellowship halls, classrooms...it's like coming home. I remember one day, when it was raining too hard to ride outside, I rode my new banana seat bicycle down the shiny polished hallways of our church. My whole life was filled with church, the Bible, and God. I loved church. I loved God. My parents believed in Proverbs 22:6, "Train up a child in the way he should go; even when he is old he will not depart from it." At nine years of age, I was baptized and knew all I wanted to do was be a "good girl" and make my Daddy proud of me.

;

Three days before my eighth grade year began, we moved from Tennessee to Texas. It was a hard move for all of us, but especially for Mama and myself. Daddy was focused on his new job; he was going to work at a large church with several staff members. He was the song leader/worship director and for the first time was not involved with the youth group. My brother was in elementary school and made friends quickly. He was also tested for the gifted and talented program which set him up with a core group of students and friends with whom he would eventually graduate high school. Mama missed her garden and her flowers. Leaving the lush green of middle Tennessee to live in the desert of West Texas was a terrible shock for her. We also had no place to live. Texas was riding the wave of a large economic boom and the infrastructure couldn't quite keep up. There were no houses or apartments available when we pulled into town, so the Holiday Inn was our home for several weeks.

Of my family members, I had the worst transition into this new adventure. My school in Tennessee had less than 500 students from kindergarten to twelfth grade. Mostly white, I can only remember a handful of minority students in the population. The junior high school I transferred to in Texas had over 1,000 students in just two grades, and the population was basically divided into thirds: white, Hispanic, black. It was incredibly stressful for a girl who was terribly shy and knew absolutely no one on the first day of school. The halls were crowded and I could hear faint conversations in multiple languages, but I was totally alone. It seems that first days of school are regulated and documented by last names. My first name was, and still is, often mispronounced. Instead of Marnie, I'm called Marine, Marie, Maxine, Marty, and the list goes on. The "W" starting my maiden name placed me class after class in the back corner of the room, surrounded by boys. Tears and fear were my constant companions; I even remember my dad offering me a reward if I could just make it through all my classes in one day towards the end of the first week. Luckily, I was a good student and my teachers seemed to like me. Early on, I received a perfect score on my math test and all those boys quickly wanted to be my friend. It was rough, but I slowly began to make friends and settle into my new surroundings.

;

Though school improved for me, church was another issue. I never quite "fit in" with the youth group. It was hard to break into the clique when most of the members had known each other for a long time. To make matters worse, the youth minister's daughter and I did not get along. She was the "Queen Bee" of the junior high kids and didn't want me changing the way things were. I tried to work around her, but it wasn't easy since our fathers worked together. Our parents were forever putting us together and trying to get us to be friends. Once, her parents even invited me along on their vacation. She was probably mortified, but put on a good front for her parents. It was awkward to say the least, but we were able to be friendly without being real friends.

Where I failed making "girlfriends," boys were another matter. Boys were easier for me to be around. I was a tomboy growing up and loved hanging out with my daddy. I was usually more interested in doing the things he liked to do. In fact, it was hard on me when I liked a guy because he knew me first as a friend and didn't want to ask me out on a date. I had very little luck with relationships early on, but desperately wanted to be "loved." Why I felt this way is still a mystery to me. My family loved me (and still does) with a type of "super" love. My entire life has been filled with affection and "I love you's" which have been translated recently into daily text messages and every love emoji in existence. I can only think in hindsight that I craved that same kind of love in the relationships outside of my family dynamics. One boyfriend I dated over and over again through middle school was the typical breakup and makeup type. He would like me just long enough to find someone he liked better and then dump me. I was so desperate to be liked that I continued to put up with his unacceptable behavior. There were several boys in the youth group I "went with" but none lasted very long. I wanted so badly to belong -- to have those relationships that looked easy for the other kids to have, but at which I failed miserably.

A SHAKY FOUNDATION

High school changed the way I looked at relationships. I started dating boys outside my faith. Most of them were very nice and treated me better than the boys at my church, and that was when I began to make a shift in my beliefs. I was coasting spiritually; proud of my ability to hang out with "the unchurched" and not be influenced by their sinfulness. I pointed fingers at the youth group, ridiculing them for their self-righteousness, while at the same time, boasting about my own abilities to reach out to everyone. I was a hypocrite.

Rarely do things blow up all at once when you start down the road to destruction; it's usually a slow boil that leads to the final damnation. My parents taught me right from wrong, but I was too comfortable in my false sense of Christian pride. I toed the line in so many ways and didn't do the things my friends were doing. I went to church, listened to the sermons about "avoiding sexual immorality," and wanted to be "good." But really, what do those things mean? Was it really a big deal? Couldn't I still be a good girl if I wasn't "going all the way" with someone, but pushing the boundaries every chance I got? I wasn't having S-E-X...or was I? I was drawing lines in the sand, walking right over them and drawing new lines. In hindsight, I can see I was out of control before anyone knew it. I was just really good at hiding my secrets, even from myself.

Then everything changed senior year. I started hanging out with my neighbor across the street. She was new to the area the summer before our final year began and we became friends. She was sweet, with a bubbly personality, and a thing for cowboys. These boys didn't ride horses or ride bulls -- they just wore Wrangler jeans and Justin Roper boots. They were a rowdy bunch who drank, dipped snuff, smoked, and cussed. For some strange reason, I fell in love. I can't explain it, but I was drawn to this crowd like flies to honey. I still have a picture of four of those cowboys sitting on the front of an old pick-up truck behind the agricultural building at school that year. I dated three of the four boys in that picture and was proud of my ability to pick and choose from the group I hung out with. In fact, I went to the last homecoming game without a boyfriend and left with one. I dated a lot of different boys that first semester of school; most without my parents' knowledge. I was just having fun.

Then Jeff walked into our group.

A year ahead of us, Jeff graduated from our cross-town rival the year before and hung out on the fringe of our group. He started showing up in the school parking lot in the afternoons, coming to the parties I was going to, and making himself known to my crowd of friends. He was cute, confident, and a smooth talker. When I think about the things he said to get my attention, I wonder how I could have been so gullible, but I was naive and desperate to have someone for my own. I should have wondered why someone who'd graduated ahead of us still wanted to hang out with high schoolers. But I got swept up emotionally and soon became Jeff's girlfriend.

I don't want to talk a lot about Jeff. To be honest, his part of this story is only a side note. Not because he doesn't matter, but because the issue isn't WHO I allowed to change me, but WHY I allowed myself to be changed. Jeff was no different from so many young men today. I see them and their girlfriends and shake my head. Some things never change.

Jeff was a classic example of the bad boy who needed fixing. He didn't have a job, or more accurately, didn't keep one. He had no direction for his life, and his grandmother bailed him out of too many situations to count. He did what he wanted and answered to no one. He lived with his mom and stepdad but they didn't expect anything of him. They had little to say or do with his life. He basically just existed. This, by the way, is never good boyfriend material. Don't make excuses for people – it makes you blind to the truth.

NEVER SAY NEVER

I never intended to have sex before marriage. It was something instilled in me for as long as I can remember, and I wanted to be a virgin when I finally met "Mr. Right." Believing I'd found Mr. Right gave me an excuse to cross all kinds of barriers I thought I had in place. I don't believe that sin is one of those things you wake up to one morning and say, "Hey, today I'm going to forget about everything I know to be right and take the wrong path." In Genesis, we read the story of the first sin. I have a feeling that Eve wasn't expecting the serpent to come across her path that day in the garden. She was minding her own business and Satan picked on her weakness, her human nature. He knew what she wanted and said to her, "You will not surely die. For God knows that when you eat of [the tree] your eyes will be opened, and you will be like God, knowing good and evil" (Genesis 3:4-6). So Eve ate from the tree and put her own desires before God's.

Satan is the father of all lies and there is no truth in him (John 8:44b). In 2 Corinthians 11:14, Paul states that "Satan disguises himself as an angel of light." He uses what he can against us, and when something doesn't work, he'll find what does. I never had any desire to drink or smoke or do drugs, but I desperately wanted to love and be loved by someone. I had an emptiness I wanted filled, and I thought a boy could give me what I was searching for. I should have seen that I was just substituting temporary happiness for real joy. That happiness was so short-lived because I suffered from such guilt and remorse. I was living one big lie, but couldn't find a way to stop. For me, sex was a drug. Once I crossed that line, I couldn't find another way to make me feel loved. I can only imagine what drug addicts feel when they are tethered to an unnatural high. Sex was my own personal addiction, and living with the guilt was my own personal Hell.

I've often asked myself how I could have been so stupid? Why didn't I see what I was doing to myself, to my family, to my future? But we live in the moment, and when we're young we think we'll live forever and never get caught doing anything wrong. We're so wrapped up in ourselves we can't see past our own selfishness. I'm not sure it will ever change. The apostle Paul agreed when he wrote, "But I am afraid that as the serpent deceived Eve by his cunning, your thoughts will be led astray from a sincere and pure devotion to Christ" (2 Corinthians 11:3). I see the deception in young people today and sometimes they see it in each other, but they rarely recognize it in themselves. I can tell you what you're doing wrong or how you're messing up your life, but I can't see what I'm doing to myself or to others around me.

It's so easy to deceive ourselves. It doesn't happen all at once but gradually. We draw lines in the sand; until there is nowhere else to go except into the abyss. It's crossing the line and telling yourself, "Okay, I'll

;

never do that again," and, in no time, finding yourself in the exact same circumstance. I made the mistake of thinking I had everything under control. I thought I was a "good girl" and God wouldn't let anything bad happen to me. I clung to all the things I didn't do: I didn't smoke, I didn't drink, I didn't do drugs. I wasn't openly rebellious. I went to church every time the doors were open, said my prayers, loved my family, but none of it was good enough. None of it mattered. I was blind to my own darkness. I was lost in my own pain.

Then reality hit.

;

Chapter 1 - Questions & Reflections:

I always focused on the things I did *right*, not the things I did *wrong*. What are the things you would point out that make you "good"? Be honest with yourself... what is your persistent sin?

Can you remember a time when you made a shift in your belief, whether positive or negative, that set you on a different course? If hindsight is 20/20, what can you see from that situation now?

List 3-5 things you said you'd never do, but have done. Circle the positive ones. Are there any negative things in the list you need to stop doing? Ask God to give you the wisdom and strength to let them go.

Jesus used a parable to speak to our tendency to be hypocritical. *"Why do you see the speck that is in your brother's eye, but do not notice the log that is in your own eye? How can you say to your brother, 'Brother, let me take out the speck that is in your eye,' when you yourself do not see the log that is in your own eye? You hypocrite, first take the log out of your own eye, and then you will see clearly to take out the speck that is in your brother's eye"* (Luke 6:41-42). In what instances have you been hypocritical of others without realizing your own failings? If you haven't already, ask God's forgiveness and for self-awareness to keep from doing it again.

CHAPTER 2

FACING REALITY

Jeff knew I was pregnant before I did.

My menstrual cycle was perfect; I was never late. When I missed the first month, then the second month, I kept telling myself I was stressed. I'd just graduated from high school, was getting ready to start college, and was so worried about starting that I freaked my body out. I was sure I wasn't pregnant; I wouldn't even take a test. In the 1980's the tests were less reliable, and I couldn't just walk into a drugstore and pick one up. The idea that I might be pregnant shouldn't have been so ridiculous to me. We never took precautions; it was never planned. After the first time, I remember telling myself, "It's not going to happen again; I can stop before we get that far." That never worked. In Jeff's defense, he never pushed me, but was more than happy when I gave in to the desire over and over again.

In the beginning, Jeff was excited about the possibility of the pregnancy and decided to tell his parents. They weren't happy about the situation, but weren't surprised either. His parents figured if it happened, we would get married, and if it didn't work out, we'd get divorced and move on. Needless to say, that was not what I wanted. I wasn't thrilled that Jeff had told his parents, especially since I hadn't taken any tests to determine if I was actually pregnant. I wanted to believe I was sick or that it was just a fluke. I held on to the lie I told myself -- swimming in a river of denial. I didn't want to tell my parents. I feared disappointing them and having to figure out what it all might mean for my future.

;

Two more months passed, but it would be only a matter of time before the choice was taken from me. By the middle of July, we were getting ready to leave on my senior trip. To avoid ruining our time together, I decided to wait until we returned home to reveal the truth of my situation.

THE APOCALYPSE

Worst. Day. Of. My. Life.

It had been a great vacation, but I knew (or thought I knew) how bad it was about to get. We returned home on a Saturday, and I decided Monday would be the best day to tell my secret. I remember calling Jeff and telling him to come over because I was going to tell my mom that I was pregnant. He didn't want to come, and can you blame him? I told him this was about us, that he'd helped me get this way, and he better get to my house instead of trying to hide from my parents.

Daddy was at work and Mama had the day off. I can still see her standing in the kitchen, washing dishes as Jeff and I sat down at the table in the small dining room situated between the kitchen and living area. Before the words formed in my mouth, the tears started.

"Mama, I need to tell you something."

She turned from the sink, worry masking her face. "Honey, what is it?"

"Jeff and I think I'm pregnant."

The look on Mama's face broke my heart. It was as if someone had punched her in the stomach. All the color drained from her features, and a look of total disbelief covered her. She asked me if I was sure. I told her I was four months late and relatively sure. She then said some things I had not expected. Mama was the one who was always controlled, calm. This news caused her to lose the composure I was so used to seeing. She screamed at God and asked how He could have let this happen? Hadn't she been a good mother and taught me better? She couldn't understand how I could have allowed myself to get into this situation. It was one of the saddest and scariest moments I've ever witnessed.

;

At this point, I lost all control and began to weep openly. Jeff was crying quietly, and I was terrified of what my father would do when he found out. Daddy was the one who got loud when he got angry. If Mama was worse than I had ever seen her, what would Daddy be like?

Mama turned on Jeff. "You'd better not be here when her father gets home," was all she said. I don't remember him leaving...he was just gone. Mama then told me she would go to the church office and tell my father what I had told her. She did not want to call him home and worry him, but she wouldn't allow me to go with her either. My brother, who was about fifteen at the time, came into the room with his shoes and left with my mother. I didn't know he'd been listening, but I think he understood that Mama needed his support for what she was about to do. As they left the house, Mama asked me, "You won't do anything to hurt yourself while we're gone, will you?" I often wonder why she didn't just take me with her, but I think she needed some distance from me. I told her I wouldn't and sank into the couch.

They were gone for a long time. It seemed like an eternity, but I believe it might have only been an hour or so. What I didn't know was that my mother actually passed my father on the road coming home early, and she motioned him to return to the church office. When they got to the building, she called in his best friend, the singles' minister, and laid out what had happened at home. My father's first words were, "Is Marnie okay?" When my mother assured him I was, he wanted to go to the house, but Mama insisted they talk some more before they headed home.

Meanwhile, I was rocking back and forth on the couch, full of fear, but all cried out, until I heard the car doors slam outside. Through a fresh set of tears, I watched my father walk into the living room, sit down beside me and hug me. He asked if I was okay and told me he loved me. He said he'd always worried that something like this might happen; that I loved too much and gave too much of myself to others. Then he said, "You've been making bad decisions; now it's time to start making good ones. We're a family, and we're going to do what's right." I didn't know exactly what that was going to entail, but I was willing to do what I could to change my circumstances. Telling my Daddy I had let him down was the hardest thing I had ever done. I was exhausted from all the lies I had been living and wanted to change it all back again.

Before long, Daddy had to return to work. When he left, my mother and I cried together. I'm not sure I've ever cried as much as I did that day. Later in the evening, when my father hadn't returned home, I knew something was wrong. I was afraid I had hurt him so deeply that he didn't want to be around me, that he couldn't stand the sight of me. I was so ashamed of what I had done to my family. It hurt so much to see them suffer for what I had done. When Daddy finally did come home, he looked as if he'd been "run through a ringer." He sat at the table, sad and broken. I climbed into his lap, like I'd done all my life and said, "All I ever wanted to be was my daddy's little girl." He wrapped his arms tightly around me and replied, "That's all I ever wanted you to be." We held on to each other, crying and saying "I love you" over and over again.

Serious Situation

Within a day or two, my family and I settled into the new norm -- the "after" that would always exist in my life. Our emotions were broken and raw like the skin of a freshly scraped knee. Nerves were shattered, tears ever brimmed our eyes, and the guilt was suffocating. I was so bound up in my own grief it was difficult to see the weariness that enveloped the rest of the house.

As a family, it was decided that I would speak to one of the ministers at our church. Daddy wanted me to seek counseling but knew he couldn't be the one to give it to me. It's my belief that he felt, incorrectly, that he'd already let me down. His best friend agreed to talk to me about my options. I'll never forget the moment I sat down in David's office. I am ever thankful for his honesty and compassion. He was shockingly candid and spoke to me without judgment or accusation. He knew how much my parents were hurting. David was the one my father leaned on, for days on end, as he tried to get through his workweek. He always treated me with love and respect.

We began our session with the discussion of what my options were considering my present situation. David laid them out like this:

"The first thing you can do is have an abortion." Sitting in the church office, I was almost speechless. How could he even say such a thing?

"Abortion isn't an option for me. There is no way I would even consider it!"

"I understand. But I want to be honest with you. Legally, you can have one. I'm not saying it's the right thing to do. It's just a fact. I want you to understand all your options. Even the ones I may not agree with."

Next, he told me I could marry the young man I was dating, have the baby, and possibly enjoy a good life. It would be a struggle. I wouldn't be able to start college like I had planned. Jeff wasn't a believer, and David explained how that could and would cause problems down the road, but it was another option. He then added that if Jeff and I couldn't make it work, we could get divorced and I would have to essentially raise the baby on my own.

The next option was to have the baby and not get married. Being pregnant wasn't the best reason to stay in a relationship and certainly not something I had to jump into. I needed to be sure it was what I wanted, and I could choose to raise the baby on my own without marriage in the picture.

Finally, David told me I could have the baby and give it up for adoption. He explained that there were plenty of people in the world that wanted to adopt children. I could be assured that my child would be well-taken care of, and I could find a way to move on and still have the life I had planned for myself. He spoke of Christian homes for unwed mothers -- places that would allow me to live, be cared for, pay for my medical expenses, and be removed from people's whispers and judgment.

We talked in depth about all my options, and I told David I wouldn't say no to anything, except abortion. I would take the time to think, pray, and research all my choices and then make my decision.

Jeff actually made the decision easier for me.

;

DECISIONS, DECISIONS, DECISIONS

My parents had basically banned Jeff from our house. He wasn't interested in coming around much anyway and didn't push the issue. I became a recluse and didn't want to go out much or do anything with anyone. During our relationship I had mostly rejected my friends to be with Jeff, so when he was gone, I was alone. Most of my "friends" didn't understand the big deal about my pregnancy anyway. They were moving on with their lives, making their own plans. One of my closest girlfriends from high school verbally attacked me when she found out I was contemplating adoption as an option. "There is no way I would ever give up my child. How could you even think about doing that?" Her righteous indignation was hard for me to handle during those fragile first weeks of indecision. I found myself moving farther and farther away from my past and tried to focus only on the future.

My parents and I made an appointment to travel out of town and visit one of the maternity homes for unwed mothers. One night before we left, Daddy asked if I wanted to go out and see if we could find out what my friends and Jeff were doing while I was home alone. I appreciate my father doing this for me. I know it may seem underhanded, but I believe he knew what kind of person Jeff really was and wanted me to see for myself. We took his car and drove "the strip" looking for my old group of friends. We found them all parked together, hanging out like I would have been if I'd not been pregnant, and there was Jeff, right in the middle of everything -- laughing, drinking, arms around other girls -- without a care in the world. I'm usually a forgiving person; I let things go on longer than they should; I overlook the bad in others and make excuses for them. But when I've had enough, I am done. That night opened my eyes to the lies I had been telling myself about Jeff and our relationship. I knew then we were over and that I wanted no more to do with him. Now all I had to decide was what I was going to do with the baby growing inside me.

The drive to the maternity home was surreal. I didn't know what to expect when we got there. At the time, the home had only one house of girls (sixteen in all), but another house was under construction next door that would provide for another group of sixteen girls. The waiting list was long and they were having to turn girls away. I had no idea a place like this existed. Back in my hometown, we didn't see teenage girls who were pregnant in school or anywhere else – they were sent to another location for schooling. I was the only one I knew who'd been dumb enough to get caught by my circumstances.

We toured the home and met the house parents. The counselor explained the Christian adoption process. Basically, they would pay for my room, board and medical expenses, and when the baby was born, I would sign over my rights to the adoption agency for them to place my baby. It would be a closed adoption. I would not know anything about the parents who would receive my child and they would know little or nothing about me.

After several hours, we got back on the road to return home. All that was left to do was pray and make a decision.

It didn't take long for me to realize that adoption was the best option for me. I knew I didn't want to marry Jeff, and I didn't want to raise the baby on my own. I wanted what was best for my child and knew that we would struggle if I tried to keep the baby at such a young age. Thankfully, my parents were very supportive. They told me they would support any decision I made, but the decision had to be mine to make. No one could do it for me. And Jeff had made it clear he wanted nothing to do with the decision. I didn't want my parents to suffer any more than they already had, and I wanted my child to have all the opportunities life could give. For me, living at the maternity home seemed like the best choice.

This was not an easy decision to make, but it was the right one for me. I knew it would be the hardest thing I ever did, but I had to make up my mind and stick to it. There was no turning back because wishing it were another way wouldn't make it so. I took a leap of faith and committed 100%.

MESSAGE TO THE MASSES

With the decision made, the next item on the agenda was talking to the church. Because of my father's position as a minister, I knew I needed to set the record straight with the elders of our church and the church family as a whole. This was going to be difficult, mostly because I felt humiliated and guilty and didn't want to cause problems for my father where he worked. Some might think it was no one's business what I had done, but I knew trying to keep it a secret would only cause more problems.

The Bible tells us to "confess your sins to one another and pray for one another, that you may be healed" (James 5:16), and "if we confess our sins, he is faithful and just to forgive us our sins and to cleanse us from all unrighteousness" (1 John 1:9). Healing, forgiveness, and cleansing sounded good to me. I knew I might have to stand up in the face of rumors and whispers, but I was ready to deal with the fallout.

Let's be honest -- there's no place rumors fly faster than in church. We hide behind the disguise of prayer, but really, we're just gossiping in the face of our own hypocrisy. How many times have you had someone come up to you and say, "We need to pray for Susan. Now let me tell you why..." And if you're a good Southern woman, you'll throw in a "bless her heart" for good measure, while you shake your head and "tsk, tsk" under your breath. That's one of the things that turns people away from the church. We can't embrace others because we're too busy pointing fingers.

When we met with the elders, we were greeted mostly with love, forgiveness, and understanding. However, there were one or two who responded with righteous indignation and holier-than-thou attitudes. One of them actually said he was glad he didn't have to worry about any of his children being caught up in the same type of situation. The fallacy in his thinking was absurd. Just because kids are in the youth group doesn't mean they aren't doing what the world is doing. In truth, they need more training on how to spot sin in their own lives and what to stay away from, instead of assuming they're going to "do the right thing." They need clear facts and brutal honesty. Good kids do bad things. It's human nature. And with all honesty...they had no idea what their kids were doing all the time...we'd been in the same youth group and I'd seen them make choices no worse than mine. But I kept my mouth shut. This was about me, not anyone else.

;

I decided that I would write a statement for the elders to read before the church the following Sunday evening. I wanted everyone to know that this was my sin; that I had made this decision on my own. My parents had raised me to know what was right and wrong, but I had chosen badly. I wanted to absolve them of any contamination by association and set the record straight.

I was in such a fog that night. I remember walking to the front of the church with my family during the invitation, sitting on the front pew, and hearing one of the elders read my letter to the congregation gathered in the building I had grown up in.

> *Dear Family:*
> *Because of the influence of my worldly friends, I have been involved in immoral acts with my boyfriend, who is not a Christian. The pain and suffering have been great on me and my family.*
> *I have asked for forgiveness from God and my family, and I ask for your forgiveness and prayers now and in the coming months as I deal with the consequences of my sin.*
> *Thank you for your strength, love, and support through this trying time in my life.*
> *In His Love,*
> *Marnie*

When I look at these words now, I see how my sin was covered up by the generalizations and shift in blame. If I wrote the same letter now, it would be more blunt and mention only my part in the scandal. After all, scripture tells us "on the day of judgment people will give account for every careless word they speak, for by your words you will be justified, and by your words you will be condemned" (Matthew 12:36-37). But I realize at that time, this was what the church was prepared for me to say and how I should say it.

My father also wrote a statement that he read aloud to the congregation. I'm not sure I even heard the words when he spoke them the first time, but reading them now brings tears to my eyes. The pain and sadness I brought on my family was almost more than I could bear.

;

Brothers and Sisters,

Glenda and I come tonight to stand beside our Marnie in this hour of trial. We share with her the responsibility for what she has done. We want you to know that we love her without reservation. We ask that you also love her and we ask that you will pray for all of us now and in the months ahead.

We bow before our Lord Jesus, and we praise the Name of our Heavenly Father for the cleansing blood of His Son, for it is only by His grace that we stand.

Tim and Glenda

What more could anyone ask for? My parents loved me "without reservation". The most often quoted scripture in the Bible is John 3:16, "For God so loved the world, that he gave his only Son, that whoever believes in him should not perish but have eternal life." God loves us without reservation. He sacrificed His most prized possession for our salvation. Jesus willingly gave Himself up for our sins, so we can have a second chance (or more) to make our lives glorify God. My parents were giving me a glimpse into that kind of love. I was so grateful; not only for my family standing with me, but for the grace and mercy of a loving Heavenly Father. However, I did not know what to expect from the church. Would they support me? Love me? Show me grace and mercy? Or would they shun me and possibly my family? As the final prayer was spoken and the congregation dismissed, I sat on the front pew, exhausted by the ordeal and fearful of what might come next.

The response of my church family overwhelmed me.

It seemed as if everyone in the building came to the front of the sanctuary to speak to us. Men shook my father's hand and patted his back. Women hugged my mother and murmured quiet words in her ears. And then, one after another they came to me. Some in tears. Some with loving smiles. Some with quiet hugs.

And then the words I never thought I'd hear:

"We are so proud of you."

"You're doing the right thing."

"We will be praying for you."

"We love you."

"I wish I'd made your choice instead of the one I made."

"You'll get through this; I did."

"You're not alone."

"I've been where you are."

"I didn't make the right decision all those years ago."

"No one knows I did the same thing when I was your age."

There is no moment like the one when you realize others are just like you. There is healing when people share your pain. We all make mistakes and live with the consequences. "All we like sheep have gone astray; we have turned -- every one -- to his own way; and the Lord has laid on him the iniquity of us all" (Isaiah 53:6). This beautiful church family embraced me and loved me because they knew what it was to be broken, shattered into pieces that only God could put back together. They understood redemption and forgiveness. They had walked the path before me and found a way to shine a light into my darkest hour. I will never forget the strength and power of that night. It made leaving for the maternity home easier and my choice for adoption more sure. For the first time in months, I was at peace.

When we got home from church that evening, my mother shared her amazement at the number of women who had confessed their secrets to her that night. So many had either had abortions or were thankful they had never been in the same situation because their fathers would have disowned them. They were shocked by my father's attitude because it was so different from the way they thought theirs would have responded. The reality of my blessings began to overshadow my fears of the future.

;

CHAPTER 2 - QUESTIONS & REFLECTIONS:

When have you had to face up to a bad decision? How did you handle it? Is there something in your life now that you need to "come clean" about? Who do you need to talk to? Stop what you're doing and make a plan - ask God for help.

When have you been truly surprised by how God has shown you His love?

What story do you have that could help someone else who's hurting? Spend some time in prayer asking God to show you the person you need to share with, then *"be strong and courageous. Do not be frightened, and do not be dismayed, for the LORD your God is with you wherever you go"* (Joshua 1:9).

CHAPTER 3

WORST WEEKEND EVER

It wasn't long after the church announcement that I packed my bags and got ready to move to the maternity home for unwed mothers. I didn't want to wait. First, because I had yet to visit a doctor, except to have blood work done to confirm my pregnancy, and second, because I wanted to get away before I really began to show. I didn't want people to have a visual memory of my pregnant belly. You might wonder how I kept my pregnancy a secret for so long, but I was very small and didn't really start showing until almost the end of my fifth month. Also, I was blessed with zero morning sickness.

Mama and Daddy moved me on a Friday. I didn't take much with me since I would be sharing a room with three other girls. I had a twin bed, a small chest of drawers and some space in the closet. That was about it. I moved into the original house, but knew it would be temporary until we were shuffled to the new house when it was completed. My parents helped me unload my belongings and put them away. We said our goodbyes and they left. I don't recall a lot of tears, but I was nervous. I didn't know anyone, and I was "the new girl." I focused on the idea of my parents returning the following Saturday. They promised to come every week to see me since I would not travel home until after the baby was born. This was September. The baby was due in January. It was going to be a long four months.

Late Saturday morning, a family friend who had recently relocated nearby came to the house to pick me up. Most girls were at the home anonymously, but I didn't feel the need to hide my identity. I understood

;

why some of them needed to, but the home offered protection, a buffer to the outside world, and I had a short list of approved visitors. Yvonne and her family drove me around town, showed me some of the "sights" and took me to lunch. We made plans for them to pick me up the next morning for church. During the night, I woke with severe cramps, and made it to the bathroom just in time to get on the toilet, grab the trash can and pray for the illness to stop. I'd never remembered feeling the way I did that morning. I didn't understand what was happening. One of the girls ran to get the house mother who came to my aide. After several rounds in the bathroom, I was finally able to lie back down. I heard whispers among the other girls that I might be having a miscarriage and there was talk that the doctor might need to be called. I remember drifting off to sleep, wondering what was happening to me. Fear of losing the baby never crossed my mind. I was so sick, I just wanted the pain and vomiting to stop, and I wanted my mama. I'd never been sick away from her cool hands on my forehead, and her constant bedside vigils. She always had a wet washcloth for my face, a deck of cards, and a game of rummy to keep my mind off any discomfort. It was miserable being without her in that moment. Before long, the house mother returned to my bedside and woke me to share a phone message. My friends from the previous day had called to say they couldn't pick me up for church because all five of them had food poisoning! We found out later, that the restaurant where we'd eaten had received tainted meat and the majority of customers who ate there on Saturday were violently ill. I was relieved to know the source of my ailment, and spent the rest of the weekend in bed.

I didn't see Yvonne or her family again while I was at the maternity home. I made a decision early on that it would be better to remove myself from all our earlier acquaintances. Yvonne was a very sweet woman. She had been one of my Sunday school teachers at church growing up. When she heard about my pregnancy, she and her husband offered to adopt my child even though they had three boys of their own. They were willing to raise and love the child, but have an open adoption with me so that I would be able to see and be a part of his or her life. She told me that the child would always know that I was the birth mother.

;

Though her offer was heartfelt and tempting to me, I couldn't do it. I knew that giving the child up, but being able to see him or her anytime I wanted would be too much for me to bear. I also didn't think it would be fair to Yvonne, her family, or the child growing inside me. I needed a clean break.

I've heard of several open adoptions that work well, and I am so happy for those families. It is a blessing to be able to watch your child grow and receive the level of love and care that you want for him or her. At this time in my life, it just wasn't the right option for me. I knew I had to let go.

When I made my decision, no more discussion was necessary. In my mind, it was already done.

It's how I survived.

A Day in the Life

I've lived with sixteen pregnant girls; I can live with anybody. Seriously! To call it a crazy house would be an understatement. There were so many different girls living under the same roof, it was like an episode of a reality T.V. show.

We had girls from all walks of life, backgrounds, and ages. When both houses were full, there were girls from thirteen to twenty-six years old; black, white, Hispanic; married, single, and divorced. During my stay, we had one sweet girl with special needs about sixteen years of age, who didn't really understand why she was there or what she'd done to get pregnant. We had prima donnas and divas who made us miserable, and girls who'd just made bad choices and were trying to make the best of their situations.

Some girls came from as far away as Washington state and their families could not come to visit them. Long distance calls and letters helped them stay in touch. Others lived close by but their parents refused to see them. One of the saddest cases was a young girl, about fourteen, whose parents dropped her off and basically told her to never come back home. There was the young girl who had decided she would give her child up for adoption, only to have her mother come to the hospital and force her to keep the child. Then there was Laura. She was the first friend I made at the maternity home. Like me, she was a preacher's kid, but she was only 16 and engaged to the father of her baby. She and her boyfriend talked on the phone all the time and still planned on marrying when she returned home.

My room was the last one in the house, Room #4. My three roommates and I got along better than any other group. We became fast friends and depended on each other to maintain our sanity through this experience we all shared. Two of my roommates, Amy and Beth, were on baby number two. Amy had been pregnant at fourteen, married at fifteen, divorced at sixteen and pregnant again at seventeen. She didn't want to give this child up but knew she couldn't handle having two children at such a young age. Amy finished her GED while living with us and saw her little girl as often as she could. Beth had a child at home that had yet to turn a year old. She missed her child's first steps because she was living away from her family with us at the maternity home. My heart broke for her missing that milestone in her daughter's life. Beth also liked to push boundaries and fought against the rules of the house, she even snuck out a few times after curfew.

My closest roomie, Darla, had traveled from another state because her family didn't want anyone to find out she was pregnant. She was supposed to be visiting relatives or off at school so no one would know. Darla and I had a lot in common. We were both loud and obnoxious girls and our family lives were similar. Darla used to sit and sing to her stomach and talk to her unborn child. She thought she might keep her baby and told God if He didn't want her to, He'd have to make it clear to her. About a month before she delivered, her mother flew in to see her and told Darla that her best friend was pregnant. Darla's boyfriend was the father of this child as well. She took this as her sign from God and changed her mind about keeping the baby. It was hard on me when she left. I had depended on her and still had two months to go when she moved home.

Girls came and went through a revolving door. We were all in various stages of pregnancy. When one delivered, she'd come back from the hospital and within a few days, or weeks, be gone. Her bed would only stay vacant a day or two and a new girl would move in. Terry, 14, had been raped while stoned at a party. She was such a sweet girl with so much innocence in spite of her circumstances. Five months into her pregnancy, she went into premature labor. The baby died two days later. She named him and buried him before she left. "At least I know he's in heaven with God. Now I don't have to worry about him living on Earth." She showed great strength, but what a hard thing to live with at such a young age..

Though we were living four to a room, sixteen to a house, we were well taken care of. We had sweet house parents and stuck to a simple routine. We had chores to do, and each room rotated meal duty and cleaning schedules. Sometimes getting new girls to pitch in was difficult, but we made do.

Throughout the week there would be excursions to the mall and classes offered at the pottery house where we could make ceramics. Some girls were able to complete classes for school so they didn't get behind while away from home. I took a correspondence course from one of the local universities, and one Saturday my parents brought my car so I could get a job and get time away from the house. Working for a temporary work service I was able to find short-term work around town and earn a little money. The independence was good for me and made a huge difference in my mental health. Most of the girls just hung around the house and didn't have anything to occupy their time. This was before cell phones and the Internet. We didn't have video games, Netflix or social media to distract us from our situation. We watched soap operas and other daytime television. Some of us completed needlepoint projects and latch hook rugs. Others put puzzles together and worked crosswords. Sometimes the monotony, alongside the hormones, made the girls cranky and argumentative, but for the most part we all tried to get along.

I was the lucky one.

A few girls' families visited once or twice in the course of their stay, but my parents came every weekend I lived at the home.

Saturday mornings, my father and mother would pile in the car, drive two hours to pick me up, and take me out. In the beginning, it was hard to see the pain in their eyes when they saw my growing belly. Over the weeks, we settled into our new normal. I could breathe and relax when they were with me; I didn't have to be on guard every moment like when I was alone. We'd have lunch, go to the mall, sit back at the house and visit. Then around dinnertime, they'd kiss and hug me goodbye, climb into the car and make the return trip home. They never missed a Saturday visit. If they couldn't both make the trip, one of my parents was always there for me. I can never thank them enough for that huge sacrifice.

Holidays were the hardest on everyone. We celebrated three big holidays during my pregnancy: Thanksgiving, Christmas, and New Year's Eve. Most girls were alone during the holidays. Phone calls were made, but long-distance was expensive, and there was only one phone per house. For Thanksgiving, my family came to visit me. Daddy checked us into one of those weekly stay hotels with a kitchenette. Mama fixed the whole holiday meal, and we spent time together as a family, but it wasn't the same. Two weeks before Christmas, I called my parents and asked if I could come home for the holiday. My parents agreed, we got permission from my doctor, and Daddy flew in to drive me and my car back home. I had been having a rough time at the maternity home for the last several weeks and felt depressed. My closest friends at the home were gone – all having delivered their babies ahead of me – I was lonely and scared. The reality of having a baby was sinking in and I wanted to be with my family.

When I got home, we decided I would stay inside and away from visitors. I didn't want people to see me pregnant and thought it was best to keep a low profile. Knowing someone is pregnant and seeing the actuality of the pregnancy are two different things. No one would know I was home, and we'd enjoy the holiday in our own house. It was good to sleep in my own bed, even for just a few days, but the burden of my situation came crashing down on me just before Christmas day. Sitting at the dinner table I burst into tears – terrified of the unavoidable future. I realized I wasn't afraid of having the baby but of giving up my only chance of being a mother. I had always wanted children, and now I was preparing to give this child away to strangers. Mama looked me in the eye and said, "This will not be your only child. I will have other grandchildren by you. The Lord will see to it. You are doing the right thing." I knew she was right but the fear remained. Just before the New Year, Daddy bought a plane ticket for me. I'm surprised they let me on the plane almost nine months pregnant, but the flight was quick and I arrived safely back at my temporary home. I had three weeks left.

BIRTH DAY

Having a baby can be a frightening experience. Not only the fear of raising a child and all that goes with that responsibility, but the actual labor experience can be scary -- especially for a very young woman who has never been in the hospital before. Most of the girls were bothered just by the regular doctor visits we had to attend. Imagine having your first "well-woman" check as a young teenager without any prior discussion or information about what to expect. We were nervous, uncomfortable, and humiliated in some cases. It was difficult to adjust to, even though it was a necessity.

As far as the actual labor was concerned, no one really explained what it was going to be like and there was fear that we wouldn't know what to do when it was time. I don't remember any Lamaze classes or information videos for us to watch. Luckily, God's perfection has instilled in all women a natural instinct for having babies, and your body takes over. Nine months is a long time to get used to an idea of what is coming. In the early months you may have fear or apprehension, but those feelings are replaced by the desire to be rid of your pregnant body.

My due date was mid January. The weekend before I went into labor was the only weekend my parents didn't come to visit. Texas weather laid a heavy blanket of ice all along the plains between my hometown and my current residence. My parents called Friday night and I told them not to risk coming along the dangerous roads. They hated not coming, but knew it was the safest choice.

At this point, I had a whole new set of roommates. I was the last of my original group to give birth. Everyone else had gone, and I'd watched lots of new girls move into the house. I was past my due date and ready to move on.

The baby's gender was going to be a surprise. Back then, doctors only did sonograms if something was wrong, and I'd had an ideal pregnancy. No illness, and I felt good. One of the girls who lived in the room next to ours was sick every morning for the entire nine months. We would hear her get up, throw up, and then go about the rest of her day. I can't imagine what that must have been like for her. It was hard enough to listen to her struggle each morning.

Another week passed and as Friday rolled around again, I began to have cramps and my back started hurting. When I realized I was going into labor, I called my parents immediately. My house mother was getting ready to take me to the hospital, and I told them not to come the next day. When they began to protest, I told them I didn't want them in town when I had the baby. I knew it would be hard for them to stay away, but I also knew it would be better for all of us if they had no chance of growing attached to a child whose life they could never be a part of. I told them I would call when it was all over. I'm sure that was one of the most difficult nights for my parents. The hours of silence that followed must have been deafening.

I got to the hospital around 10 p.m.

At first, the doctor didn't want to admit me. I was just starting contractions and had no other signs of labor advancement. I used my stubbornness to tell the doctor and nurses I was already a week past my due date, and I was not going back to the home. They finally admitted me around midnight. What came next seems comical in hindsight, but was far from funny when it actually happened.

The nurses administered a shot of Demerol to help calm me down. My blood pressure was high (something I would have to learn to live with eventually), and I think they wanted to help me relax as we waited for my body to move through the stages of labor. We didn't know I was allergic to Demerol. With most people, the medication calms them down and allows them to rest during contractions. It has the opposite effect on me; I get aggressive and belligerent. Not a good combination. I think I may have told one of the nurses stroking my arm that if she didn't stop touching me, I would rip out her arm and beat her with it....I can still see her face. I would apologize to her, but I'm sure she'd heard all kinds of things in the delivery room. I'm not one to be "petted" when I'm hurting anyway. Not long after that, they administered my epidural.

The epidural didn't work the way it was meant to. I was unable to move the lower half of my body. I couldn't pull my legs up; I couldn't feel anything. When we got to the actual delivery, I didn't even know when to push. The doctor had to read the machine attached to my abdomen to know when a contraction was coming to give directions for when I should push. It was difficult at best and far from an easy delivery. When the baby was finally born, I asked if it was a boy or a girl. The nurses acted as if, because I was giving the baby up for adoption, I didn't have the right to any information. Reluctantly they told me I'd had a boy. I felt like the medical personnel treated me differently because they knew I was "one of those girls."

I was exhausted, and my brain was fuzzy from exertion and medication. As the doctor was attending to my physical needs there was a noise from behind me. His head turned toward the door of the delivery room and he said, "Ma'am, you can't be in here!" The reply that came was music to my ears.

"I'm staying. She's not going to go through this alone!"

My friend, Yvonne, came to my bedside. Somehow she had heard I was having the baby and came to make sure I was okay. She was tiny but mighty. I can only imagine what she said and did to get herself into the actual delivery room. She stayed with me until I was taken to a private room where she contacted Deanna, to keep me company. Deanna was a few years older than me, from our youth group back home, and was attending a local university. We were not close friends, but she came and slept in my room all night. She gave me food and drink when I was flat on my back waiting for the epidural to wear off, and she helped me back and forth to the restroom. She even stayed with me when I saw my son for the first time.

I can never repay these two women for what they did for me.

I am forever in their debt.

Chapter 3 - Questions & Reflections:

What would you consider the worst day you've experienced? Was it one of your making or someone else's? How did God bring you through it?

In my experience, people tend to fall into two categories: they see the glass ½ empty (negative) or they see the glass ½ full (positive). Which type of person would you say you are? Why would you say that about yourself? Ask someone close to you how they see you. If they say something different than you did above, ask them what traits or actions show them that side of you.

Take some time to talk to God thanking Him for His blessings and asking Him to help you change your perception (if needed) so you can praise and glorify Him in all things. *"Count it all joy my brothers, when you meet trials of various kinds, for you know that the testing of your faith produces steadfastness"* (James 1:2-3).

CHAPTER 4

My Son

Let me tell you what I know about my son. He has ten fingers and ten toes. The toenail next to the pinky toe is shaped like mine and my father's. He has dark hair and big inquisitive eyes.

He is perfect.

I held him the evening after he was born. The nurses brought him to me; I fed him and changed his diaper. I loved him and kissed him. The next morning, early, they brought him back to me.

I held him, told him I loved him, and let him go.

As the nurse pushed his bassinet out of the room, my case worker from the adoption agency came in with papers for me to sign. I remember thinking that this was a defining moment in my life, one of many "semicolon pauses" to come, and I was ready for it to be over. I was asked more than once if I was ready to sign, if I understood what I was doing, if I was completely sure this was what I wanted.

The answer to all those questions was "no."

The answer I gave was "yes."

I signed my name and gave up my child.

I thanked God for the strength to do it.

"Go get the doctor," I said. "I'm ready to go home."

Going Home

My parents had called while I was still at the hospital, expecting me to have to stay another day or so. They had left home right after morning church services to visit me. I had just finished seeing the doctor and he was getting ready to release me, so I told them to stay at the home because I would be headed there shortly. I made a deal with the doctor. I knew I didn't want to stay in town if I didn't have to. I told him my parents were in town and that I wanted to go home; I begged him to let me go back with them. After some discussion about the two hour trip, laying down in the car, seeing my family physician at home and returning in six weeks for a checkup, he relented.

My housemother was there to shuttle me back to the home. We drove into the garage, I shuffled slowly into the kitchen, and my parents leapt from their seats in the living room to greet me. I didn't stop moving. My mother said, "Honey, why don't you just sit here and rest for a moment?" motioning to an overstuffed chair in the living room.

"The doctor said I can go home. I'm going to pack my stuff."

"What? The doctor said you could leave?"

"Yes, and that's what I want to do, now."

Through tears of relief, Mama and Daddy helped me to the back of the house where my room was located and helped me pack my meager belongings. I was so tired. I barely remember getting in the car and tilting the seat back. The next thing I knew, I was walking into my house on the arm of my father. He walked me to his big recliner and gingerly sat me down.

There are no words to describe how good it felt to be home.

ON THE ROAD TO RECOVERY

Through a haze of pain medication and weariness, I heard my mother tell my father, "You've got to go to the store and get her some things. I am not leaving my baby!" At the time, I didn't understand what she was talking about until almost an hour later, when my father returned with two bags from the local store. He had every type of feminine product you can imagine. That sweet man had stood in the aisle and read the packages of all the different types of items, even talked to a woman who was shopping at the time (I wish I could have seen her face!), until he was sure he'd gotten exactly what I needed. He was so proud of himself. He felt so helpless in my discomfort; I know he wanted to get me whatever I needed to feel better. It's a memory I cherish.

Recovery was slow. I'm not sure I got the best care at the hospital. It was old-fashioned in its approach to a lot of things, but my mom took great care of me when I got home. Two weeks later and my first outing was to church Sunday morning. I wasn't sure how people were going to react to my being back. They knew where I'd been, but hadn't seen me pregnant. I just didn't know what to expect. One of the sweet women came up to me that first Sunday, sat down by me on the pew, patted my leg and asked if I was doing okay. She said no one would think bad of me if I cried; that it was okay to be sad. I remember thinking, "I could cry every day for the rest of my life about the loss of my child, but God is in control, and I'm not going to do that."

Things were different after I returned -- most of my friends were off at college, or had moved away. I'd separated myself from the youth group and didn't really fit in with them anymore, and the people I would have hung out with, I kept my distance from. Four or five weeks after the baby was born, Jeff showed up at my house wanting his "things" back. He had the audacity to drive up in a shiny, new pickup truck with a girl in the front seat with him. I was home alone, both my parents were at work, and when I answered the door, I was unprepared for his smugness. He said he could come back at another time if I couldn't give him his stuff right then, but I told him to wait, that it had all been packed up for some time. He took the box from me and walked back to his truck. He didn't ask about the baby. He didn't ask how I was doing. He just climbed into the truck and backed out of my life.

THE LIST

I'd promised the doctor when I left the hospital, I would return in six weeks for my check up. This was also the time when the adoption agency would give an exit interview to the birth mothers, a way to have some closure to the adoption process. I've mentioned before that I didn't want an open adoption because I wanted some distance between the family and myself. I didn't want to know who they were, or where they lived, but knowing absolutely nothing was difficult.

A few months before my due date, I had written a letter to my child. The adoption agency said they would include it in the baby's file and give it to the parents. The parents would decide when they thought it was the right time for the child to read it. I have no idea if he ever got it. Part of the letter reads:

> *My dear child,*
>
> *...It is not your fault that I got pregnant without being married, and that is why I decided to have you. I've made a grave mistake, but I can give you a chance of a good life by giving you parents who can take care of you and give you all you deserve. I'm now eighteen and will be when I bring you into this world. My love for you is so strong, that I'm sacrificing what I want for what is best for you. If I could, I would keep you myself and raise you as best I could, but that is not what you need or deserve. I want you to have the best in life, and I believe that will come with a mother and father who can take care of you the right way.*
>
> *If, when you're older, you ever want to find me; I'll be happy to see you. If you do not, I'll understand. I know that as time goes by you might be perfectly happy with your family, and I hope that for you. But if you do want to see me, I won't deny you that right. I love you, and could never turn my back on you!*
>
> *In case you're curious, I plan to name you for my own purposes. You will not be called by the name I give you, but by the name your parents give you...if you are a boy I'll call you Gabriel Joseph. The meanings are why I picked those names in particular. They are derived from the Hebrew language meaning: "the Lord is my strength" and "He will add."*
>
> *I hope that life brings you nothing but happiness. Please remember that I will always love you and I will never forget you!*
>
> *In my heart always.*

;

I also wrote a letter to the adoptive parents and found an appropriate card to send with it. The outside said, "You've Adopted Someone Special" and inside read, "May life hold worlds of happiness and many blessings, too. For you and that sweet little one who's come to live with you." Then I added these words:

> Dear adoptive parents,
> My child has been given to you with a great deal of love already bestowed upon it. I know that you will love it and care for it all the days of your life, just as I would have done if I had been able to keep it. I'm giving up my rights to this child because I feel it is what is best for my child. If you had not wanted a baby, then you would not be adoptive parents. I thank you from the bottom of my heart for opening your home and letting my little one come into it. I only gave my baby life and birth, but you are the ones who can give it a life to live and enjoy for years to come. Please take good care of my child, and let it know that my love and thoughts are with you and your family. God bless you always!
> In His love.

When I first decided to give my son up for adoption, I'd spent a lot of time in prayer and created a "grocery list" of items I needed to feel at peace about my decision. I wanted him to have a mother and father who were not able to have children of their own and really wanted a little boy to complete their family. I wanted him to have an older brother or sister who would look out for him and take care of him. I wanted his parents to have a nice home and enough money that he would never want for anything. I wanted them to be Christians (that's why I'd picked this specific agency), and I wanted him to have the same physical characteristics as their family.

After we visited the doctor, and I got a clean bill of health, Mama and Daddy drove me to talk to the adoption counselor. We sat in her office while she gave me some "non-identifying" information about my son's adoptive family. This is what she told me:

- they'd been married 12 ½ years

- they could never have children
- they adopted a little girl five years earlier and wanted a little boy
- they were "superb" Christians (I'm not sure what this means.)
- they lived in a large Metropolitan area
- both graduated college
- they made good money
- they had a nice home
- he worked for a large utility company
- she was a teacher
- both had brown hair, brown eyes and olive skin (like my son)
- their daughter loves him and shows gentleness toward him
- they are proud of him and he's doing just fine
- he'd grown in the six weeks they'd had him and was a good baby
- he was a wonderful completion to their family

Every petition I had asked God for was answered. I walked out of the agency for the last time, tears in my eyes, a smile on my face, and the heavy burden on my heart lifted by God's mercy. For the first time in my life I understood the words of Jesus: "Ask, and it will be given to you; seek, and you will find; knock, and it will be opened to you. For everyone who asks receives, and he who seeks finds, and to the one who knocks it will be opened. Or which one of you, if his son asks him for bread, will give him a stone? Or if he asks for a fish, will give him a serpent? If you then, who are evil, know how to give good gifts to your children, how much more will your Father who is in heaven give good things to those who ask him!" (Matthew 7:7-11)

After that day, I never questioned whether I did the right thing or wallowed in self-pity about my decision. I think about and pray for my son often, but I don't worry about him. I know God is a better provider than I could ever be, and He is watching over my son -- wherever he may be.

HELPING HAND

People deal with life-changing situations two ways: they try to forget about it and act like it didn't happen, or they take the lesson they learned and try to help others. I wanted to help other girls who found themselves in a similar situation. Over the next few months I had the opportunity to talk to a handful of girls who were pregnant and wondering what they were going to do. Ministers or family friends sent them to me. One girl chose to have an abortion. I was so angry with her; I couldn't speak to her after she'd had it done. To be honest, I was a little self-righteous back then. I felt like she'd slapped me in the face, though I realize now I shouldn't have taken it personally. It's a decision she's had to live with. I tried to help the ones I could. I talked with them, shared my story, but mostly just listened to them.

Women and girls in this particular situation feel very alone. The ones I met with were scared, confused, and angry. They had questions and fears of the future ahead of them. Some gave up their children for adoption and others kept them. I know of one family where the daughter couldn't take care of the child, so the grandparents took the child and raised it. I offered a shoulder to cry on and tried to be a friend when they needed one. It was something I thought God wanted me to do. I had a story to tell and people who needed to hear it, but I let them come to me, quietly and in hushed tones. We talked behind closed doors or whispered over telephone lines.

It was all I could do.

I thought the past was behind me.

Chapter 4 - Questions & Reflections:

What is something you've really prayed for and how did God answer that prayer? Why do you think He answered like He did? Or are you still waiting for Him to answer?

Some people think God is a genie in a lamp that you rub to get what you want. But John 15:7 tells us, *"If you abide in me, and my words abide in you, ask whatever you wish, and it will be done for you."* (Abide -- "to remain stable or fixed in a state" or "to continue in a place.")[2] What do you think this means in reference to your prayers? How does abiding change the things you pray for or how you pray?

What is a problem or topic that you can speak to directly that might help someone going through a similar situation? What is holding you back from sharing how God has changed your life?

---

[2] "Abide." Merriam-Webster.com Dictionary, Merriam-Webster, https://www.merriam-webster.com/dictionary/abide. Accessed 28 Feb. 2024.

PART 2; LOSING MY RELIGION

"Wash yourselves; make yourselves clean;
remove the evil of your deeds from before my eyes;
cease to do evil, learn to do good..."

Isaiah 1:16-17a

CHAPTER 5

NEW START

Begin again. Clean the slate. Turn from your sin. In theory, we all want an opportunity to start again. We'd like to be able to pick ourselves up, dust off the grime of our past and point ourselves in a new direction. It was time to get my life back on track.

In my house, the question was never "Are you going to college?" but "Where are you going to college?" I knew it's what my parents wanted, and I decided to go somewhere I thought would make them happy. I'd screwed up a tuition-free college scholarship at our local community college because I'd been giving birth instead of taking classes. My parents had met at a Christian university in Tennessee, and I thought I might "clean up my act" by attending a Christian college as well. There were several within the state of Texas I could have chosen, but I didn't take the time to look into them or do any research. The internet wasn't a "thing" yet and unless you drove to a campus for a physical tour, you wouldn't know what you were getting into. The closest Christian university was where a number of the former youth group members were attending. I had no desire to follow in their footsteps. The only other university I was familiar with was Harding University in Searcy, AR. I was only looking at Church of Christ schools and my search was limited. I was making rash decisions and trying to make things right without thinking about the consequences. I was still trying to work it all out on my own -- not seeking God's counsel, but making assumptions based on my own ideas. I should have followed Proverbs 3:5-6, "Trust in the Lord with all your heart, and do not lean on your own understanding. In all your ways acknowledge him, and he will make straight your paths." My Christian maturity was definitely lacking.

I settled on Harding because it was far from home, and I believed I could start fresh. It is probably one of the poorer choices I've made. Not because there was anything wrong with the school but because it was the worst choice for me. I was too far from home and I had zero support. I was miserable and wasted my parents' money on a directionless C average. I went to chapel because I was forced to, attended church because it was expected of me, and felt smothered by the rules and regulations of a conservative university. I was angry at the world.

I was also still looking for love in all the wrong places. A smart person would turn from their broken ways and remember what brought them to this point in the first place. But like the Israelites of the Old Testament, I ate the bountiful manna from God one morning and woke up complaining about it the next. I couldn't see how I needed to change in order to make my life different. I allowed life to happen to me, instead of setting a course for my future.

"Better the devil you know than the devil you don't."[3] This phrase speaks to my mental and emotional fear of moving beyond my failures and making a true change in my behavior. The only real way to make a new start is to acknowledge the sin and failure, confess it, and move on in a new direction. I had publicly confessed, but never really dug down to the root of my sin to find a way to reform my mind and heart. I thought a change of scenery and determination alone could keep me from making more mistakes.

Even though I wasn't completely where I needed to be, God still used me while I was on campus. One night, I was walking across the commons with my roommate and two other female students. No one knew about my past here. I'd kept a tight lid on it because I wanted to leave it all behind, but that night, for some reason, I told them all my story. One of the other girls burst into tears. She explained she'd been raped just a few weeks before when she'd gone home for a friend's birthday party. She'd

---

[3] "Better the devil you know than the devil you don't." Merriam-Webster.com Dictionary, Merriam-Webster, https://www.merriam-webster.com/dictionary/better%20the%20devil%20you%20know%20than%20the%20devil%20you%20don%27t. Accessed 28 Feb. 2024.

just found out she was pregnant and didn't know what to do. After our talk, she called her mom and they removed her from school. We learned that she moved to a maternity home and gave her child up for adoption. Years later, she asked me to be in her wedding because we'd shared something few could understand.

God was working on me, but I wasn't listening.

My second semester at Harding, I began corresponding with an ex-boyfriend from high school, Michael. He'd gone into the military after graduation and was what I latched on to in my loneliness. We got engaged that spring and I thought all my problems were solved. I was miserably in love. I couldn't wait to return home to make wedding plans and take another vacation trip with my parents and younger brother. Interestingly enough, we were headed back up the East Coast. It was my brother's trip to tour universities before his senior year and my excuse to spend time with my fiancé.

We traveled to Virginia Beach so I could spend a few days with Michael, and then moved on to Washington, D.C. As a family, we toured some of the capital's landmarks, but I was sick with missing Michael. My parents knew I would make the rest of the trip unbearable, so Daddy bought a bus ticket for me to go back to Virginia Beach. The plan was for me to spend several days with Michael, staying at his friend's house, then ride across the state to meet my family on the way home. Thinking back, my parents shouldn't have let me have my way. I know I was over eighteen and most would say they didn't have the right to tell me what I could or couldn't do, but they were financing my life and I was lost in so many ways. Maybe they didn't know, but I still lived with them and desperately needed direction. I hadn't changed. I wanted to, but I was still gripped by insecurity and weakness. It would have been better for me to stay with them and work through the pain and loneliness I feared. Instead, I returned to my old self and sought comfort and love through sex.

The bus ride across Virginia to meet up with my family was a metaphor for my life at the time. Starting out from Virginia Beach early in the morning, the ride was supposed to last six hours but turned into an all-day event that never found me at my destination. The bus broke down in the middle of the trip, outside of a small convenience store in the middle of nowhere. After a two-hour wait, a new bus was delivered and broke down when it pulled in front of the gas pumps. Another wait, another bus, and several hours later, we pulled into the town station before my final stop. I had been able to contact my parents along the way (which was a miracle in itself since I had to rely on payphones and landlines). They drove an hour out of the way to pick me up ahead of my destination. It was one of the longest days of my life. I should have spent some time reflecting on what I was doing – I was headed in the wrong direction. I should have seen God's hand at work, showing me what I was doing with my life – He was throwing up road-blocks and I was driving through them. I should have opened my eyes to the road of self-deceit I was traveling. I foolishly thought all my problems were going to go away, but I was pushing past warning signs, headed to the cliff's edge, and had no idea what God had in store for me.

Michael and I had planned to get married the following March. While making wedding plans, working full-time, and trying to figure out what I wanted to do with my life, I started getting cold feet. It wasn't that I didn't want to marry Michael; I loved him. What I feared was leaving my parents' house and going straight into my husband's house without knowing if I could survive on my own. I had a hard enough time keeping my life together with my parents paying for everything. I knew I wasn't ready. When I called Michael and told him I wanted to move the wedding date so I could spend some time on my own, he'd been drinking, got verbally abusive, and threatened me. That finally got my attention. I broke off the engagement and sent the ring back. Michael wasn't a bad guy. I don't believe he would have followed through with the words he spoke in anger, but God used him to push me in a different direction. I thank God everyday that he gave me the wisdom in that moment to walk away from that relationship.

Regardless, I still hadn't learned how to control my feelings. I jumped from one shallow relationship to the next – always desperate for someone to love me, find me important, and desirable. I was living a lie, " outwardly appear[ing] beautiful, but within [was] full of dead people's bones and all uncleanness...outwardly appear[ing] righteous to others, but within [I was] full of hypocrisy and lawlessness." (Matthew 23:27-28). I was trying to find my way, so I went back to school, took some classes at the community college in town, and made better grades than before. I thought I had it all under control, but control is a lie Satan uses to mislead us. Without relying on God, control is fleeting and temporary.

In the fall, my brother left for the University of Texas in Austin since he'd been given a full-ride scholarship to study with the honors program. He was the golden boy; I was the black sheep. (This is one more lie of the enemy, but it's how I felt at the time.) When my brother left, he never looked back. He came home to visit, but he had dreams, plans, aspirations, and none of them included moving back home. His leaving put me at greater odds with myself. I felt like I needed to get my life back on track and get out on my own. When I traveled to Austin to visit him during his first semester, I fell in love with the city. I'd never been much for bright lights and the pulse of a town that rarely slept, but Austin called to me. I wanted to throw off the shackles of my past and start over. I wanted to be somewhere new and be someone new. I was ready to reinvent myself, again. Maybe this time it would work.

Another New Start

January brought resolutions and promises, but I made friends with the wrong people. I lived on a co-ed dorm floor and hung out with a group of guys who were vulgar and irresponsible. Most nights we played cards and drank until the early morning hours. By May, I was flunking out of school and on the road to becoming an alcoholic. I thought I'd taken control of my life, but instead, I'd given control to those around me. I spent my time trying to please everyone so they would like me. I quit church because it didn't fit into my new lifestyle or with my new friends. Finally, I told my parents I was unhappy with school and didn't know what I wanted to do with my life, so I dropped out and went back to work full time. I needed to "find myself" but didn't have a clue how to start. I was drifting aimlessly, unsure what to do next. I had no purpose and no direction.

My brother and I decided to move in together, and we lived on the bottom floor of an old house right off campus. I worked a couple of minimum wage jobs and my life became a vicious cycle of working, drinking, and nameless men. There were days I'm surprised I was able to go to work. The shame I feel from those months weighs heavy on my memory. Though it is a long time in the past, Satan has a way of pulling it out of the filing cabinet and placing it in the front and center of my mind. I hate that he knows where I am vulnerable. I hate that he wants me to feel soiled and broken. I know that I'm worth so much more than I allowed myself to be during that time of my life, but sometimes the memory of my feelings of worthlessness during that time is overpowering.

During those first twelve months in Austin, I didn't want anything to do with God, and no one held me accountable. My parents would call and ask questions about church and friends, and I would lie -- lie about church and whether I had gone or not, lie about my lifestyle and what I was doing. They didn't visit often, and I didn't travel home much. At one point, I started a paper route with the Austin American Statesman to help make ends meet. It was one of the best jobs I've ever had. I'd roll out of bed at 3:00 a.m. and head to the warehouse to pick up my papers, seven days a week. I couldn't take a day off, but that was okay with me. The money was good, and I enjoyed the solitude of the early morning streets.

My day jobs changed from working the floor of a retail chain to working in the office of a department store. I liked the work well enough. It was a job and paid the bills, but none of it challenged me. I started spending time with some of the girls from work. We'd work all day and spend our evenings at one bar or another. Most nights found me close to drunk and lonely. What meager salary I made swam at the bottom of a whiskey glass. I was slowly bleeding all of my resources, and my life was spiraling out of control. Darkness covered all aspects of my life, and I couldn't see a way out of the pit.

Chapter 5 - Questions & Reflections:

When have you turned your back on God? What lies of the enemy were you listening to during that time?

What history does Satan keep bringing up to steal your peace?

When Satan tempted Eve and twisted the truth that God had told her, she and Adam turned their backs on God and hid from Him. When God came to the garden looking for fellowship with them, they hid because they were naked. Then God asked, *"Who told you that you were naked?"* (Genesis 3:8-11) God didn't care that they were naked, but Satan created uncertainty and confusion. Write down the lies you still believe about yourself. Mark them out and then write down the truth of God that dispels the lie.

CHAPTER 6

MAD AT GOD

Being mad at God is exhausting. Trying to act like everything is "okay" and nothing is wrong just makes it worse. I didn't realize I was mad. If I'd known I was angry, if I'd cried out against God and asked Him why He let some things happen, I might have had some relief. At that point in my life, I thought I couldn't question God or get mad at Him. I obviously didn't spend enough time reading the Psalms. Those chapters are full of praise and wonder, but also questions like, "Why, O LORD, do you stand far away? Why do you hide yourself in times of trouble?" (Psalm 10:1). But I held it in and fooled myself, looking for someone other than God to fill the hole inside my soul. It ate away at me like a cancer. It changed me.

I was rotting from the inside out.

That's the way my life was those years after I gave my son up for adoption. I was full of insecurity, and I wore a convincing mask of happiness and self-confidence. I don't believe anyone knew how broken I was inside. My family and I went about our lives and tried to pick up the pieces, acting like all was forgiven. Nothing had changed. Not really. Not at the core. The connection to my parents was stretched so thin, I'm surprised it didn't break and snap back to slap us across our cheeks. We played our parts and played them well. We didn't even know that's what we were doing. My family said they forgave me, and I'm sure they did as much as they could. But the poison from my decisions lay just under our skin. Like a bruise you don't remember until you hit it again; all is forgotten until the pain returns.

;

I know a story about a man who, when his son was born deformed, was so angry with God, he cried out against the Almighty. He questioned the Holy One. He said, "My God wouldn't give me a son like this!" Members of his church flocked to him, held him up and got him through his pain, until he could see the mighty hand of God working through the life of his precious little boy. Sometimes I wonder if I would have been better off to react the same. Maybe someone would have seen how badly I was hurting on the inside and would have stepped in and helped me get through my pain. Someone with the voice to wake me up and tell me to take control of my life. But instead of blaming God, I blamed myself. Instead of asking Him why, I embraced my weakness. I drank more, kept my family at a distance, and made one bad decision after another. Rather than turning toward God for answers, I turned away from Him. I wanted nothing to do with the training I'd grown up with. I wanted to do things my way. I wanted to be free from what I thought was the condemnation and hypocrisy of the church.

What I didn't realize was I had never truly repented of my sin. Repentance means you make a change. I didn't change how I lived my life. I felt remorse for what I'd done, I sought forgiveness from my family, the church, and from God, but I didn't know what that really looked like. I regretted the things I did. I thought I could resolve to do better, but it was beyond me. In my childishness, I didn't understand true repentance and I had no concept of godly sorrow. "For godly grief produces a repentance that leads to salvation without regret, whereas worldly grief produces death" (2 Corinthians 7:10). Worldly sorrow was slowly killing my soul. I had a shallow relationship with God, built mostly on my parents' teachings and the generational faith of my family tree. I took it all for granted.

I foolishly believed I was the master of my fate.

I thought I was having a good time, living life free of the constraints being a preacher's kid had put on me. I thought my life was my own and no one could tell me what to do. So I drank away my inhibitions, and gave myself freely to whatever man would show me affection, unaware of the long-term effect my sin had on my heart. The Bible refers to the umbrella of sexual sin as sexual immorality and warns of the damage it can cause. "Flee from sexual immorality. Every other sin a person commits is outside the body, but the sexually immoral person sins against his own body" (1 Corinthians 6:18). My heart grew cold and black, callused by the pain and sadness I ignored.

I recently heard a pastor speak on sexual intimacy like I never have before. Proverbs chapter 5 is a direct call, warning God's people of the dangers of sexual sin outside of marriage. The pastor explained that "physical intimacy is exclusively a component of marriage." You cannot separate physical intimacy from marriage without damage or destruction to the relationship. God created this intimacy when He created marriage in the Garden of Eden, making our bodies, male and female, to fit together perfectly through this physical intimacy of marriage. God created us and He created this intimacy for us. It is His, and only He fully understands the way it works. Because it belongs to God, the pastor explained that God "infused physical intimacy with supernatural spiritual power. [It's] not benign, it's alive, it's living...because God invented physical intimacy to bring one man and one woman in a relationship called marriage for life, in the deepest, oneness relationship between two humans on this side of heaven." That's why the Bible says a man and woman will become "one flesh" when they are united in marriage (Mark 10:8). It is a reflection of a Christian's relationship with Jesus. The act of physical intimacy knits the souls together as one. So when you have multiple partners or sexual intimacy outside of marriage you leave pieces of yourself behind. It's only through God's grace and forgiveness that we can reclaim those pieces and be made whole again.[4]

If only I'd understood the depth of my actions back then, and the years of pain it would cause me in the future, I might have been able to change my course and lessen the number of scars I carry.

The beginning of the end came in December 1991. I'd been throwing newspapers for about six months and every morning I listened to a local radio show. Those morning personalities can be so gregarious and over-the-top. I enjoyed listening and one day decided to call in. Every

---

[4] Nathan Lino (August 6, 2023) *Proverbs 5: Part 1* FBCForney App [Online Video]. Available from: firstbaptistforney.sub-spla.sh [Accessed: March 20, 2024]

morning they'd tell us what the weather was like outside, but this morning they were way off the mark. I called in to give them a hard time. When I told them I was a "papergirl" they jumped on it, and I became a regular on the air. I'd throw my route, call in, and give them my "from the street" weather and comments. They'd introduce me: "It's Marnie, the PAPER-GIRL!" It was one of the best parts of my day. Then, one morning, I called and they put me on hold for longer than usual. Routinely, they'd talk to me off air and then say "Okay, your segment is coming up" and then switch me live. This time I just waited. It was as if they'd forgotten me. I was frustrated and hurt. It seems so silly now, but I was angry. I hung up and called back. When one of the guys answered the phone, he said, "Hey Marnie, what happened? You weren't there when we got to the phone." And I said, "Well, you kept me on hold for fifteen (expletive) minutes!" Both of the guys in the booth got quiet then one replied, "Wow, Marnie, that was LIVE." I didn't know what to say, I mumbled "sorry" and hung up the phone. I should have known then how bad my life had gotten, but I was too blind to see my own stupidity and self-destruction.

In January, one of my friends told me about a clerical opening at the university. I applied and got the job. For the first time, I was in a position with regular hours and retirement. I could walk to work and stay in the city I loved. The job was split between two offices within the same building. I worked in the graduate office, sending out and receiving packets of information for admissions in the mornings and then moved upstairs to manage the clerical work for several of the professors within the department. I worked the giant machine we used to copy dissertations, took phone messages for professors, and sent out preliminary information cards to students all over the world interested in attending our program. For the first time, I really enjoyed work. I made different friends, mostly mature women who were married with kids. These ladies weren't interested in going out to the bars or partying. That first month I was still seeing my friends from my old job, but it was becoming less frequent and less enjoyable.

Then one morning, sitting at my desk in the graduate office, I got the worst case of heartburn I ever had. I began to panic and thought I was

;

going to be ill. I asked my supervisor if I could leave a little early for lunch and headed to the nearest pharmacy for some antacid. As I chewed the chalky tablets, I began to count in my head, then scoured my brain. I was sick with fear. Lunch was forgotten.

It just wasn't possible.

It couldn't happen.

God wouldn't do this to me.

Not again.

I pushed down the panic rising from my disbelief and went back to work. I tried not to think about it. I tried to forget the last time I had heartburn.

Two weeks later, I was sitting in an abortion clinic, waiting to pee on a stick.

;

Chapter 6 – Questions & Reflections:

When have you been mad at God? Was it because He did something you didn't want Him to do, or because you believe He didn't come through for you like you wanted?

I had a Bible study teacher tell me once that when we think either of those things we might as well tell God to get off His throne because we think we can do better. Spend some time in prayer right now asking God to forgive you of your pride and ego and thank Him for being in control of the life He's given you.

Explain a time when you've been so far off track that you've made a fool of yourself in front of others. How did it make you feel? Did it wake you up or did you ignore the warning signs in front of you?

Has your soul been torn in pieces by the sin of sexual intimacy? God can restore what is broken and give you peace. Take some time right now to confess those times and ask God to heal your soul so you can be fully one with the spouse God has given you or will give you in the future.

CHAPTER 7

Wake Up Call

I can still see the clinic. The ugly beige walls. The claustrophobic waiting room with its crumpled magazines and sliding glass receptionist window. The "homey" couch where I sat with my counselor after they called my name, and I walked through the door dividing me from my life before. I remember feeling anxious – sweaty palms and frustration. I remember thinking, "Let's get this test done, appointment made, and get out of here and on with my life."

I got something else instead.

I got Sue: a meddling, middle-aged woman who wanted me to talk about my feelings. I got a woman who knew way too much about me and my situation. I got someone who wasn't pulling any punches. She wouldn't let me take the test and run, like I wanted. She made me sit and talk to her. She asked me questions, and like a dog with a bone, wouldn't let me quit until I gave her the answers she wanted. The real answers, not the lies I told myself. She asked me why I wanted an abortion? Why was I doing this to my parents, to my family? Why had I turned my back on God? She went into graphic detail about what the abortion would do to me both physically, emotionally, and spiritually. She cut to my core with softly spoken reprimands and promises. When pathetic answers fell from my mouth, she picked them up and turned them on me with love and compassion. She told me God loved me; He had a plan for me. He didn't want me to have an abortion. He wanted me to know all the costs.

I told her I couldn't do this again. I couldn't go through a pregnancy and give a child up for adoption. I didn't have the strength to give another baby away. She said I didn't have to. She told me God would give me the strength and ability to raise this child on my own. I thought she was crazy. She didn't know me! How could I tell my parents? They would be devastated. Their anger and pain would be more than they could bear. How could I be a part of that? How could I make it okay with them? What was I supposed to do?

She told me it would all work out; God was in control. I'm not sure I believed her.

Her advice to me was to go home and write a letter to my parents. "Be brutally honest with them," she said, "then sleep on it." When I woke the next day, I was to read it again and make changes if needed. When it was exactly like I wanted, I should mail it and know God was going to take care of me. I figured it couldn't be that easy. But when I promised I would do as she said, she finally allowed me to take the pregnancy test I'd come for in the first place.

I recall her explaining how it worked. It wasn't like the modern stick tests. I had to collect a urine sample, apply a drop to the plastic encased square and then drop the activation liquid on top. If the test was positive a large + sign would appear in the small window. She tried to explain that we would have to wait a full five minutes for the activation to work, and no matter how light the plus sign was, it would be a positive result. As I came out of the restroom with my cup in hand, she collected the test pieces together. As she prepared to drop the activation liquid on the test strip, she reminded me that it might take up to five minutes. I already knew what the answer was. As soon as she applied the chemical, a large black positive sign appeared, like someone had taken a thick, black marker and marked an X on the spot. She said it was the fastest, darkest, positive sign she had ever seen. I just nodded my head and said, "I don't do anything half-way."

I gathered my things and went home.

For the first time in a long time, I prayed. Fear and sadness overwhelmed me. The shock of what I had just been through and the gut-wrenching guilt of reality hit me like a truck when I got to my bedroom. The realization of how far I'd fallen from where God wanted me to be was too much for me to bear. I was totally broken. I thought I knew this road from my previous choice with Gabriel, but this path was much lonelier and more frightening. I realized I was totally on my own and only God could help me.

I sat down that evening and wrote my parents a letter. The last four years of my life had been a lie. I had been living apart from everything I knew to be true and right. I explained my situation, the shame I felt, and the understanding that they might not be able to handle this second pregnancy. Knowing I could not give another child up for adoption, I realized I might have to live with the loss of my family. I feared my parents might not survive the scrutiny and shame I brought to them. I told them I was going to raise this child alone, and I would love to have their support, but I also knew they might never want to see me again.

With the letter written, I slept soundly for the first time in weeks.

The next morning when I woke and reread the letter, it said exactly what I wanted it to say. I prayed God would take care of the details and mailed it.

And I waited.

It was excruciating. I paced the floor and ran through all the possible outcomes. I tried to work through what my decision would mean for me, for my child. I had no idea what I was doing. I only knew I needed to finish what I had started.

ALL BY MYSELF

Why was I going through this alone?

Who was the father and where was he?

That's not an easy question to answer, and my answer makes some people uncomfortable.

The truth is, he didn't know, and if I had my way, he never would.

Before the whispering and finger-pointing starts, let me explain. "He" was never part of a "we" except for one night. Before I ever knew I was pregnant, he was gone. Very early, he had shown himself as untrustworthy, and I saw him as a threat to my child's safety. He wasn't going to have the opportunity to ruin my child's life with inconsistent behavior.

No one knew who he was.

It was my secret to keep.

Two or three days after I sent the letter home, I got the phone call from my parents. They were not happy, to put it mildly. My mom said when she first read the letter, she thought I had simply written a poem or something for them to read. Then she understood the content, and she and Daddy got angry. This was nothing like the first time. There were no words of comfort. No tone of understanding. My father's voice came on the line and his displeasure buzzed across the miles of telephone wires.

"Do we know who the guy is?" he asked.

"No."

"Is he in your life now?"

"No."

"Is he coming back?"

"No."

"Then we won't talk about him again."

And that was that. But the fun wasn't over. My father proceeded to tell me that I could never come home after I started to show. He and Mama would not be exposed to this shame before the church again. I understood. I knew that what I had done might possibly ruin our relationship forever, but I was resolute in my decision. No matter what, I was going to have this child and be the very best mother I could be. It was time to give up "childish things" (1 Corinthians 13:11) and grow up.

The separation from my parents was a blessing in disguise. Living in Austin gave me freedom without feeling shame every time I looked at my parents' faces. I was determined to turn my life around and make better choices. Because I had decided to keep this child, I knew I had to make significant changes. For the first time, someone else was depending on me. The day I found out I was pregnant was the last day I drank alcohol for fourteen years. I had to cut off the cancerous relationships from my most recent past. My old friends drifted away quickly, unable to process my need for change and to go in a new direction. It was time to find new friends, godly friends that would hold me accountable in my new found faith, weak as it was.

;

But first, I needed to thank Sue for helping me with my decision and giving me the courage to write my parents. I wanted to tell her she'd been right about everything. As bad as I thought it was going to be, it wasn't going to kill me, and I was going to be okay. So I called the clinic to talk to her. The receptionist answered the phone and when I asked for Sue, I was told no one by that name or description worked at the clinic. When I told her I'd been there a few weeks before, she said there was no record of my appointment.

Then I knew.

God had sent an angel.

To save me from myself; to save my unborn child.

It was time to go to church.

;

Chapter 7 - Questions & Reflections:

Hebrews 13:2 tells us, *"Do not neglect to show hospitality to strangers, for thereby some have entertained angels unawares."* Take some time to sit and reflect on past encounters with strangers. Have you ever been visited by an angel? Maybe there's been a time when you realized that God protected you from yourself or a situation you were in.

Use the space below to thank God for His intervention (in whatever form it took) to safely get you where you are today.

Are there any "childish things" you're holding on to? Things you don't want to give up or think you can't give up because you've done them for so long? List them below, then ask God to give you what you need to overcome and mature in your faith. Remember that *"we are more than conquerors through him who loved us"* (Romans 8:37), and *"[we] can do all things through him who strengthens [us]"* (Philippians 4:13).

CHAPTER 8

LOST AND FOUND

I've shared this part of my testimony with all types of women, from all walks of life. Usually, I see tears or they tell me they "got chills" from this part of my story. I can understand that. Living through that moment did much the same for me. But I've also had a small number who have approached me with comments that took my breath, squeezed my heart, and capsized my calm:

"I wish God had sent me an angel."

"Why didn't God stop my abortion?"

"You're luckier than I was."

Here's the thing that's hard for me to say in the face of their sorrow, anger, and pain: maybe He did. Maybe God did send you an angel, but you didn't recognize it. Maybe He did try to stop your abortion, but you ignored His warnings. In 1 Corinthians 10:13, it says "No temptation has overtaken you that is not common to man. God is faithful, and he will not let you be tempted beyond your ability, but with the temptation he will also provide the way of escape, that you may be able to endure it.". Over and over again, I hear people use this verse and misquote its message. "God won't give me more than I can handle" is spoken through false bravado and plastic smiles. But the pain and suffering pours out of them. This isn't all the verse is talking about. Temptation and suffering are two different things.

When we are tempted, He will provide a way to get away from the temptation. As I look back on past sins (and there are many), there are times I can see doors of escape God placed in front of me that I refused to take. He gives us free will. We have an obligation to do something, to act against the wishes of the evil one. God isn't going to pull us away. That doesn't teach us anything. "For the Lord disciplines the one he loves, and chastises every son whom he receives" (Hebrews 12:6). God gives us choices, but we have to be paying attention. There are distractions and road blocks, but sometimes we are so filled up with the sinful desire, we can't or won't see past it.

He can use the things around us to give us an opportunity to choose a different path -- a phone call, traffic jam, Holy Spirit nudge, etc.. I don't always choose correctly, but in this instance I was lucky in that I finally heard God talking to me. I lived more than six years of my life in utter darkness, blaming everyone else for my own failings. But I was the one who wasn't paying attention to the countless times God provided my escape from temptation.

Suffering is different from temptation. God allows us to have more than we can handle in order to get our attention and have us rely only on Him. Sometimes we are bombarded with so much discomfort, pain, suffering, panic and fear, that the only choice we have is to cry out to God for help. Even those closest to Jesus suffered at the hands of Satan. "Simon, Simon, behold, Satan demanded to have you, that he might sift you like wheat, but I have prayed for you that your faith may not fail. And when you have turned again, strengthen your brothers" (Luke 22:31-32). Christ didn't say that Peter would not stumble, but that when he picked himself back up and returned to the Lord, he would help his fellow Christians. The stories of Job, King David, Esther, the apostle Paul, and countless others in the Bible, all have moments when they have no choice but to cry out to God. Those who are the greatest defenders of Christ, those who seem to have the strongest faith, are those who "walk through the valley of the shadow of death" (Psalm 23:4) with the Good Shepherd. They have been delivered from the fiery furnace (Daniel 3). They have been placed in bad circumstances "for such a time as this" (Esther 4:14). They have been so far down, the only place they could look was to God, and He restored them. For each of us, that darkness, that despair, that end of our rope is different. We can't judge whose story is worse. We can only be thankful for God's saving grace offered for each of us where we are. But we also have to be prepared for a different outcome. In the Old Testament book of Daniel, Shadrach, Meshach and Abednego knew that God could deliver them, but that the Almighty might have a different plan. "If this be so, our God whom we serve is able to deliver us from the burning fiery furnace, and he will deliver us out of your hand, O king. But if not, be it known to you, O king, that we will not serve your gods or worship the golden image that you have set up" (Daniel 3:17-18).

This is the hard part. This is the piece that we, as mere humans can't understand. I know my story may be different from others, and I don't want it to be a condemnation for other women. What I want everyone to know is that God has a plan, a bigger picture we cannot see, and He is in control. No matter the responses made in the past, no matter how many bad choices, and I can't say this enough: if you know Christ, God will make it okay in the end. We just have to have faith. "And we know that for those who love God all things work together for good, for those who are called according to his purpose" (Romans 8:28). The key is loving God because He already loves you. He knows what is best for each of us.

A perfect example of this love is found in Luke chapter 15. Jesus tells a story about a man with two sons: one follows his father's wishes and one decides to take off on his own. It wasn't until recently that I actually understood what the word "prodigal" meant. I always thought it meant wayward or lost. In some versions of the Bible he is called "the lost son," which made sense. But, another definition of prodigal is "one who spends or gives lavishly and foolishly."[5] He lives the high life until he loses everything and is feeding slop to pigs. It's then that he opens his eyes to what is really happening to him. He realizes how far he has fallen from the life his father wanted for him. He exhibits true remorse and goes home to seek forgiveness. Totally unworthy of his father's love, he is willing to become a slave if he can only live under the shelter of his father's house. When he is still a long way off, his father sees him, has compassion on him and runs to welcome him home (Luke 15:20). This is

---

5 "Prodigal." Merriam-Webster.com Dictionary, Merriam-Webster, https://www.merriam-webster.com/dictionary/prodigal. Accessed 10 Apr. 2024.

an exact picture of our Heavenly Father. He is watching for our return; waiting with open arms to embrace us. I had been the prodigal daughter to my parents. I had run from them and returned seeking their love and understanding. Now it was time to seek forgiveness from God. I was broken and unworthy, but He was willing to pick up the pieces, put me back together, and welcome me home.

STANDING IN THE FACE OF FEAR

I was afraid to go to church. I was afraid of what people might think of me, of what they might say, of how they might treat me. They didn't know me like my previous church family. They had no reason to love me or help me. I was stepping out into a great unknown. I had no idea what to expect, but knew I had to take the first steps to get my life back on track. I needed help and prayed for guidance.

There was a congregation right off campus and I spoke with the minister there. I told him everything – from Gabriel to the new pregnancy. This was the first time I ever laid it all out to examine it. The minister treated me with kindness and acceptance. He gave me hope that I could belong somewhere again and be loved by good people. They had a good-sized college/young adult group that embraced me and my need to belong. They didn't judge me or rebuke me. They loved and welcomed me. No questions asked; no stipulations; just open arms and warm hearts. It was exactly what I needed. "Thus says the Lord: "Keep your voice from weeping, and your eyes from tears, for there is a reward for your work, declares the Lord, and they shall come back from the land of the enemy. There is hope for your future, declares the Lord, and your children shall come back to their own country" (Jeremiah 31:16-17).

I was finding my way back home.

Maybe the maturity level is what made the difference. Maybe it was the blended backgrounds of a college town that make them more open to newcomers. Whatever it was, it was much better than my experience in the youth group I'd grown up in. It was easy -- seamless. We fellowshipped together, ate dinner together, watched movies and hung out at each other's apartments, all creating months of easy healing and restoration for my broken heart. One of my favorite memories was when we all attended "Shakespeare in the Park" along the Town Lake River during the sweltering heat of an Austin July. I was very pregnant at the time, but we spread blankets on the ground and watched a production of "A Midsummer Night's Dream." It was beautiful. Not just the play, but also the friendship that held us all together.

I was slowly finding my way back to God and finding myself again. I found the strength I needed to stand up for myself, to make better choices, and to look beyond the next few days into a future filled with hope, not desperation. I was terrified to be a mother, but every day I felt God moving in me to show me I could do this. God even helped me find the way to share my faith with others.

For the most part, the women I worked with every day were believers, both Protestant and Catholic. It wasn't that we talked about God all the time, but we could broach the subject without anyone going too far to one side or the other. It was different with the students who came into our offices. Many were from foreign countries, and I was confronted with vastly different religious beliefs for the first time in my life. We had students who followed Buddha, Islam, and a few I'd never heard of. Outside my upstairs office was an eastern-facing window where one young man came to pray every day. I had never had to defend my beliefs before. I never really thought about it. I'd lived my entire life in the "Bible Belt" where everyone went to church or at least affiliated themselves with one whether or not they actually attended. Being surrounded by all these different cultures was a totally new experience for me.

One of the guys I worked with, Ethan, was a teacher's assistant in the department and from Great Britain. He was an Atheist. We didn't talk about God until the day he walked into my office and said, "Anyone who believes in God is an idiot!" It was an interesting way to start our morning conversation, but there it was. One of the women I worked with (an older woman who was devout in her faith) literally screamed from her desk in the other room, "IF YOU DON'T BELIEVE IN GOD, YOU'RE GOING TO HELL!" Ethan and I rolled our eyes at each other and he motioned with his hand as if to say, "See what I'm talking about?"

I just looked at him and asked, "So you think I'm an idiot?"

"Well, no."

"But I believe in God. And you just said anyone who does is an idiot."

"I didn't mean YOU...but how can you believe in some mysterious being?"

I answered with what could have only come from God. "Let me see if I can explain it in the simplest way possible. If I believe in God and you don't believe in God, and there is no God...then I'm okay and you're okay. It doesn't hurt me to believe in something that doesn't exist. But if I believe in God and you don't believe in God and there is a God...well, you've only got a 50/50 chance. I'm batting 1000, so I'm good either way." Ethan opened his mouth to speak and closed it again. Then he huffed out a breath and said, "No one's ever explained it like that before. Doesn't make me want to believe, but it gives me something to think about." Then he walked out of my office. We had many more discussions after that, but we were always civil when it came to God. I never pressured him or told him he was doomed to Hell. I figured it wasn't my place to do more than plant the seed; maybe someone else came along and watered it after he went back to England. I'll never know, but I'm thankful that the Holy Spirit gave me the words to say when I didn't know what was going to come out of my mouth. Matthew 10:19-20 says, "...do not be anxious how you are to speak or what you are to say, for what you are to say will be given to you in that hour. For it is not you who speak, but the Spirit of your Father speaking through you." I try to remember this now when I'm confronted with the opportunity to share God's truth with others.

;

Chapter 8 - Questions & Reflections:

Explain a time in your life when you've taken the opportunity to share the truth of Jesus with someone.

If you've never shared the Gospel with another person, take some time to pray right now for God to give you the opportunity and ask Him to open your eyes to the people He places in front of you.

When did you play the part of the prodigal? Is there someone in your life right now who is far from God and needs your prayers to find their way home? Make a list and pray for those people right now.

CHAPTER 9

A BABY CHANGES EVERYTHING

About halfway through my second trimester, I started having problems with my pregnancy. I felt fine, most of the time, but a silent killer was stalking me. When I was pregnant with my son, my blood pressure was elevated, but as soon as I gave birth, it went back down. I've always had higher blood pressure than others my age; it's hereditary. Doctors ran all kinds of tests when I was growing up, but never really found the cause. I watched my salt intake and though my pressure measured naturally high, it did not pose a real problem. All that changed with my second pregnancy. My OB/GYN put me on medication and watched my numbers. Then one day I came home from my regular appointment in stunned silence. My blood pressure was not responding to the medication, and my doctor was threatening to put me on bed rest or in the hospital.

What was I going to do? I wasn't allowed to exercise, and with the second baby, my belly was already huge. I was working two jobs: the paper route and the university. My doctor didn't know that I got up at 3:00 a.m. and then worked until 5:00 p.m. five days a week and had the early mornings on Saturdays and Sundays. I called my parents, terrified of what might become of me if I couldn't work, and they wouldn't help me. I'd only seen them once or twice since our phone call following my letter home. I'd gone home right after the letter to visit my dentist and I'd not been back. At six weeks, I was already showing and couldn't go home again.

When I called my parents and told them what my doctor had said, they were shocked and worried. After we talked, they hung up the phone without any resolution. I continued to work, but came straight home every day and went to bed. By this time, I had moved out of the little house apartment I had shared with my brother to minimize living costs for both of us. Though he was somewhat supportive of my decision to have the baby, he was still working to finish his degree and we saw little of each other. He'd gone into a co-op and I'd chosen a less-expensive, one-room apartment. It wasn't much, but I liked it. My church friends would come and hang out in my tiny apartment to keep me company.

I returned to the doctor for a follow-up and explained my situation. Single, and working to support myself, I couldn't afford to go on bed rest. We made a plan. I would go to work, put my feet up all day, take the elevator instead of the stairs, and get a handicap sticker for my car so I could park right outside of my office building. When I got home, I had to go to bed and not get up until the morning. I never did tell her about my paper route, I was so afraid she would make me quit, and I needed the money to survive.

I let my parents know about the new plan. There was relief in their voices, but something else, too. My daddy told me he'd been wrong. He said when I called two weeks earlier and explained how sick I was, it was like God was giving him a wake-up call. He said, "God told me, 'I don't know who you think you are, but your baby girl needs you, and you better get it together.'" He and Mama had decided if I had to go into the hospital, I would go back home and be there with them. It was the breakthrough I'd been praying for. I was overcome with emotion and cried with relief. I had my family back.

My grandparents, on both sides of my family, were very conservative Christians. When I got pregnant the first time, we chose not to tell most of the family because my parents didn't want to deal with the questions and accusations that might have required explanations. My father did tell his parents, and though they loved me, there was a moment when raw emotions and tension between the generations made things awkward. With this second pregnancy, and after my medical scare, we obviously needed to let the rest of the family know what was coming.

;

I used to tell people I was as Southern as a person could get: my mama was from Georgia; my daddy was from Virginia; we lived in Tennessee, Alabama, and Texas all my life. One night I received a phone call from my grandmama in Georgia. My mother had just gotten off the phone with her, and she wanted to talk to me. If you've ever talked to someone from Georgia, especially an older person, you know how that southern drawl can drag out the words. Nothing comes quickly, but the words can cut like a hot knife through butter. My heart banged against my chest...would she cut me with her words? Would she still love me?

"Marnie, I just got off the phone with your mama."

"Yes ma'am."

"She told me you gonna have a baby, but you not gettin' married."

"Yes ma'am."

"Well, it's nuthin' to have a heart attack about, it'll be okay. We love you."

In shocked silence, I stood with the phone to my ear. I could hardly respond. We spoke a few more minutes and then I hung up. I couldn't believe how all the fear that had consumed me at the beginning of this journey was slowly falling away and being replaced by love and acceptance.

Waiting for the Big Day

For most of my pregnancy, I thought I was having a boy. Sonograms were rare, and my insurance wouldn't cover one without an emergency, so I had no idea what the baby was going to be. About halfway through the pregnancy, I started thinking of names and settled on Levi Edward. My father's best friend was named Levi. Our home had been filled with the stories of their adventures and I remembered them fondly. Wanting to honor my daddy with the child's name, I thought I'd use his friend's and add his middle name, Edward. When I told Daddy about my name choice, he was almost speechless. He asked, "Did I ever tell you Levi's full name was Edward Levi?" He was thrilled with my choice. A girl's name wasn't picked until about two weeks before I delivered. I decided then that I might need to have a backup in place, just in case I didn't have a boy. I read a couple of baby name books and couldn't find anything I was really excited about. Then I found the name Jade. It's my favorite color but also a precious stone. The name fit my situation; I would get something precious out of a "jaded" past. The middle name was easy. I would pair it with mine, Elizabeth, an old family name that both sides of my family had used. With names chosen, I was ready; it was almost time.

I moved into my last trimester, still working two jobs, but taking it easy at every opportunity. I didn't go out except for church and work. I sat most of the days away and went to bed as soon as I got home. I feared having the baby by myself again. My parents lived six hours away, and I knew they might not get to me in time to be there for the delivery. Of course, I'd done it before, but this was different. I was different, my circumstances were different, and I wanted my family with me this time if at all possible.

When I started seeing my doctor every week, my blood pressure refused to stay under control. Though I was medicated and doing everything I physically could to stay healthy, it wasn't working. Every time I went to an appointment, my blood pressure was higher than the time before. Finally my doctor told me, "When that bottom number hits 100, we are going to induce." The very next appointment, my blood pressure was 140/100. She looked at me and said, "How does Wednesday sound? It's time to have this baby."

This was another blessing from God, my last appointment was on a Friday. When I got home and told my parents the doctor was going to induce my delivery the following Wednesday, they made plans to come. My father was able to handle his church responsibilities on Sunday, then he and Mama headed to Austin to be with me. If my blood pressure hadn't been out of control, we wouldn't have scheduled the birth, and they might not have made it in time. As it was, God allowed them to be with me for the most important day of my new life.

;

SPECIAL DELIVERY

Daddy drove me to the hospital early Wednesday morning, October 7, 1992. They quickly got me into a room and set up the IV and meds that would start me on the road to delivery. My mother and brother showed up a few hours later, and we settled in to wait. Daddy spent time with me in the beginning, reading aloud to me from one of our favorite authors. He'd get quiet when the machine I was attached to started beeping with my contractions. He'd look to see if I was okay, I'd nod and say, "Keep reading!" I needed the distraction. We checked into the hospital early, before 7:00 a.m., and around noon, my brother moved down the hall to sit in one of the waiting rooms while Daddy went downstairs to find a place to catch a quick nap. None of us had gotten much sleep the night before, but my mother stayed with me in the birthing room. The anesthesiologist came in about thirty minutes later to administer an epidural to give me some relief from the pain. The doctor told Mama that I was progressing at a normal pace and if I stayed on target I would deliver the baby by six or seven o'clock that evening. The nurse left us about one o'clock to gather the needed instruments for the delivery and to check on other patients; my doctor returned to her practice across the street from the hospital.

About 1:30 p.m. I told Mama I thought something was wrong. I was feeling strange and wanted the nurse to come and check on me. She patted my hand and left the room in search of the nurse. When she found her in the hall, pushing a tray of instruments, she said, "Marnie thinks she needs you." The nurse rolled the cart into the room, saying "Look how lucky we were. There was a tray already made up, so I took it. Now let's have a look at you." As she reached for the thin white sheet that covered my enormous belly and lifted it to look underneath, her face paled.

"Don't do anything!" she yelped and raced to the phone by my bed. "Marnie needs Dr. Brown now! Right now!" and she slammed the phone down. Turning to me, she looked me hard in the eye, "I need you to be calm and don't push. Dr. Brown is on the way. Whatever you do, don't push." I know I must have looked like a deer caught in headlights. I didn't understand what was happening. Mama was flustered and confused. She rushed to my bedside and we both watched the door. In a moment, my doctor came rushing into the room, shoving her long red hair under a surgical cap. She raised the sheet across me and said, "What are you doing having this baby right now?!" Through stuttered breaths I answered, "I...don't...know!" She ran to the sink, washed her hands to the elbows and pulled on gloves. On the stool beneath me, she finally told me to push, and a few moments later, my daughter, Jade, was born.

I waited for Dr. Brown to hand her to me, but she didn't move. She sounded concerned for a moment and told me that the baby was fine, she was out, but the doctor couldn't give my daughter to me. There was something wrong with the umbilical cord. The nurses huddled around as my doctor cut the cord and freed my baby. They wrapped her tiny body in a sheet and handed her to me. My mother looked at Jade, locked eyes with me, and ran from the room.

Mama rushed down the hall to where my brother was waiting. Everyone thought we were in for a long evening and were unprepared for the baby's quick arrival. When my mother ran to my brother and said, "We have a baby girl!" he looked at her quizzically and ran to the room. Coming to my bedside, he looked at my daughter and said, "I'll go get Dad" and was gone. In mere moments, my father was by my side. They had taken Jade and placed her in the bassinet. They were weighing her and cleaning her off. The nurse looked at my father and told him he could take pictures if he wanted. It was his turn to run to the car for his camera! A three-ring circus best describes the room in those first moments. Everything was chaotic happiness.

Within a few minutes, they placed my baby girl in a clear plastic bassinet and wheeled her to the nursery to clean her up and check her vitals. Before they moved her from the room, they put special bracelets on me, the baby, and my parents to make sure there was no mistake to whom we all belonged. I was prepared to move to another room where I could rest.

My treatment at this hospital was vastly different from what I'd received years earlier. Some was due to the advances in medicine, but most was because of the wonderful staff of doctors and nurses that surrounded me those two days. My mother actually bought a cake and thank you card for the nurses on the floor after I'd been released to show our appreciation for the care I'd received.

Dr. Brown came and told me a little about what had happened with the delivery. She said that if I ever decided to have more children, I needed to let them know that I moved through labor stages faster than normal. She also said, it might be risky for me to have any more children. The reason she'd had to cut the umbilical cord so quickly right after birth was because the cord was only about twelve inches long, very short by normal standards. It also had only one major blood vessel providing nutrients for the baby. Dr. Brown said we were lucky; my daughter was small, but healthy. The baby could have suffered severe trauma or developmental issues with such a small blood supply throughout the pregnancy. I was so thankful that God had given me a healthy baby.

PAPERWORK

Soon after I was moved to my permanent room, a nurse came in with my sweet little girl all clean and wrapped up tight in a blanket. The nurse looked at my father and said, "Do you want to hold her?" Handing her to my daddy, he responded, "It's been about 20 years, but I think I still know how this works." It was love at first sight for both of them. The nurse handed me the birth certificate to fill out and left to check on other patients. After I'd completed the form, a few minutes later, the nurse returned. She glanced at the certificate as she walked toward the door and stopped. "You didn't put down the father's name."

"I know."

"You have to put down a father's name."

"No. I don't."

"I'm new on this wing, but I'm pretty sure you have to put down a name. I'll have to check with my supervisor."

"That's fine. Check with your supervisor, but I'm not putting a name down."

I said all of this with a smile on my face and with no animosity in my voice. I knew the law. I'd done my research, but my mother was panicking. As the nurse left the room, she spoke to me in hushed tones. "What are you going to do if she says you have to write a name down?"

"I'll just tell them I have no idea who the father is. It could have been John, or Bobby, or Matt, or a handful of other men."

"Oh, Marnie, you wouldn't!" my mother responded. I promise you, she looked like she might faint. I laughed out loud. "Mama, don't worry about it. They can't make me put it down." Holding Jade in his arms, my father agreed with me. "It'll be alright, Glenda." Sure enough, the nurse returned and said, "I'm sorry, you were right, you don't have to fill out the father's name." A little addled, she took the form and left.

I slept well that night, or as well as you can sleep in a hospital. The next morning I got up, took a shower and dressed in regular clothes and waited. Around two o'clock my doctor finally came by to see me. She walked in and remarked that I looked ready to go. After some discussion and a list of instructions, Dr. Brown signed my release. Jade and I could go home.

Going Home

Mama and Daddy drove us to my little apartment. My mama stayed for a short while and then she and my brother left so she could get a good night's sleep before staying the next two weeks with me. My daddy stayed that first night with us and took care of Jade so I could rest. It was a rough night. I had chosen not to breastfeed Jade. I knew I would be going back to work soon, and being a single mother, I knew I needed the ability to have other people feed Jade when I couldn't. Breastfeeding would be hard for me and wasn't encouraged then as it is today. No one really talked about it, and I don't remember it even being discussed while I was in the hospital. That first night home was tough. I was having horrible pain and paced the floor most of the night. I couldn't hold Jade and I was exhausted from lack of sleep. My daddy slept on the couch and got up every two hours to take care of my sweet little girl. By the time he got her fed, changed and asleep, it was time to start all over again. I remember crying to him as he fed her in the early hours of the morning; telling him how helpless I felt and how sorry I was to make him do so much. He just smiled at me and said, "Sweetie, this is what daddy's are for. We take care of our little girls. It's okay. You rest." I cried harder. The next morning, my pain was gone, Mama was back at the apartment for baby duty, and Daddy was on his way back home to work.

Mama stayed with me the next two weeks. Jade was born on a Wednesday, and on Saturday we went shopping. I bought her the cutest little dress, and the next morning, three generations were sitting together in the pew at my church. Everyone was so surprised to see me there only four days after giving birth. They showered Jade with compliments and affection. The next week I paid for my enthusiasm. I could hardly move; I'd overdone it. Mama took care of us over the next several days and then Daddy returned to take us home so I could continue to have help while I recovered on maternity leave. I might have been anxious about going back to the place where I grew up, but something amazing had happened over the last few months. Once my parents had accepted the fact that I was having another child outside of marriage and had determined to support me, they let the congregation know about my situation. Fearful of how they might feel about me or react to my child, I didn't know what to expect. Thankfully, my fears were never realized.

Before Jade was born, I received several cards and letters from members of our church back home. One of the most memorable cards I received was from one of the older women of our church. I knew that she was suffering mercilessly from cancer. Her body was dying from the inside out. Every day she got weaker and weaker, and yet, she took the time to write a note and send a check for $100 to help with any costs I might have with the new baby. I wept when I opened the card. I had heard how much she was hurting, but she still reached out to me. It was one of the most significant moments of my life. I will never be the same because of what she did.

It reminds me of the story from Mark 14 where the woman comes to worship Jesus and attends to him before his crucifixion. She brings an expensive jar of perfume and pours it over His head. Those with Him complain about wasted money and how it could have been better used to tend to the poor, "But Jesus said, 'Leave her alone. Why do you trouble her? She has done a beautiful thing to me…She has done what she could…And truly, I say to you, wherever the gospel is proclaimed in the whole world, what she has done will be told in memory of her" (Mark 14: 6, 8, 9). Soon after I returned home, Susan went to be with the Lord.

One of the things I couldn't understand was how some of the other ladies in our church dealt with her death. They were angry and outspoken about their displeasure toward God by allowing such a "wonderful woman" to die. It's ironic. I was rejoicing in her freedom from pain and suffering, but they couldn't get beyond their own grief. I told them what a difference she had made in my life and how thankful I was to her for her generosity. I hope it made a difference to them because she certainly made a difference in me. I want to be more like her; to show my faith in the midst of adversity. To speak up with my very last breath and show God's love. I share her story often with those who are hurting and questioning why God allows certain people to die. She was a shining example of the type of godly woman I want to be.

A NEW LIFE

Jade had her very first plane ride when she was four weeks old. My parents sent us back to Austin so I could resume work. I had intended to start back at both my jobs but soon realized I was not physically ready for both. My first morning back on the newspaper route, Jade took her 3 a.m. feeding in her car seat, bottle propped up on a stack of newspapers. The guys at the warehouse loved seeing her. They would carry her car seat into and out of the warehouse where we rolled our papers every morning. They would coo and tickle her and tell her stories. It was a great way to start our mornings together.

Previously my route had been a small neighborhood with close-in streets where I threw from both sides of my truck at once; from the driver's side window and across the front seat through the passenger side window. I threw papers every day of my pregnancy until the Sunday before my delivery date. Since I had been forced to give up that route to go on maternity leave, I was given a whole new route when I returned. If you don't think God is in the details, you aren't looking hard enough at the big picture. The new route I was given was in a more affluent part of Austin, with extra wide streets and large property lines. Before, my route only went down a street one time and zigzagged across the neighborhood. The new neighborhood route took me down one side of the street and would return to that same street later in the drive, attending to the houses on the other side of the street. Every paper was thrown out the driver's side window. I never had to subject Jade to a possible dropped paper or to the window being open right beside her tiny sleeping face.

Once my maternity leave was up, I had to find someone to watch Jade so I could head back to work full-time. I found a young mother from our church who had recently had a baby as well. Her daughter was a month or so older than Jade and she agreed to watch her when I returned to the university. I had to drive about twenty miles outside of town to get to her house, but it was important for Jade to stay somewhere I could trust and afford. Money was tight; I was drowning in debt.

The debt started as soon as I'd gone off to college in Austin. I had a truck payment and insurance, but I'd also gotten a credit card and kept it maxed out at all times. When another card arrived in the mail, I started using it too. Among the doctor bills, childcare, rent, etc., I couldn't buy groceries at the end of the month. My first cry for help went to the church. I asked for a loan to help cover some of my most pressing expenses. They graciously gave me $1000 to defray my costs with the understanding that I would pay them back as soon as I could. When that money ran out, I decided to apply for government assistance. All I wanted was food stamps, to buy formula for Jade and food for myself. I had a great medical plan with the university and I was covering, if barely, the rest of my expenses. When I met with the benefits advisor, she told me I didn't qualify for food stamps. I explained my situation, and she told me I made too much money and would need to quit one of my jobs. At first, I was ecstatic! I would happily give up the early morning paper route if I could get help to offset my growing debt. But she said no; I'd have to give up the university job in order to qualify. Dumbfounded, I looked at her. "You want me to quit the job with benefits and retirement?" She said it was the only way. "So you're penalizing me because I work too much?" She said it wasn't ideal, but it was the way the system worked. I walked out of the office despondent. What was I going to do?

That very same week, my babysitter quit. She said she couldn't handle both babies at the same time. I understood, but I was panicked. I couldn't afford anyone else and didn't know what to do. I prayed and called my parents for help. We discussed my options and Mama finally said, "If you will come home and go back to college, we will help you take care of Jade." I didn't know it then, but my parents had been talking about what was best for me and how to get us to come home so I could have help raising Jade and take solid steps for my future. Thankful for their generosity, I agreed and prepared to leave the city I loved.

The university took my two weeks notice and allowed Jade to come to work with me. They must have felt sorry for me. Each morning I would bring her in her stroller, set her up in the carrier on the table beside my desk, and start my workday. Ethan, my friend from Great Britain, would come in and tell Jade all about what he had watched on Sesame Street that morning. He loved American television and thought Sesame Street was brilliant. It was funny to hear him explain about the silly conversations between Bert and Ernie or the word of the day. Jade watched him with huge brown eyes and listened to the melodic lilt of his British accent. The other two women in the office took turns putting Jade in the stroller, pushing her around the halls of the building, and feeding her. Then after lunch, we would move upstairs to my other office where she would nap in her stroller. The ladies in the office down the hall took over feeding and rocking her. It wasn't ideal, but it was so much better than any other option I had.

Two weeks later, right before Jade's first Christmas, Daddy came and helped me pack up my tiny apartment. He drove a borrowed van, and I followed in my little red pickup, bed piled with boxes and a baby sleeping in the front seat.

Chapter 9 - Questions & Reflections:

Romans 3:23 says, *"for all have sinned and fall short of the glory of God."* Unfortunately we want to put weight on different sins to make ourselves feel better. We judge others by their sin and often treat them differently than we should. Especially when the consequences of their sin is harder to hide. Describe a time when you felt like others were judging you more harshly than you deserve. If you've been lucky enough to never feel that way, write down a time you've misjudged someone and what they are going through. What could you do in the future to see others with the same grace God sees them? Is there someone you need to apologize to and make amends with so you can restore your right relationship with God? Do it quickly!

When has someone taken the time or resources to help you when you desperately needed it? How did it make you feel?

When have you had the opportunity to bless someone else? Did you follow through? Why or why not?

PART 3;   NOBODY'S PERFECT

"All we like sheep have gone astray;
we have turned—every one—to his own way;
and the Lord has laid on him the iniquity of us all."

Isaiah 53:6

CHAPTER 10

One of the hardest things for me to grasp about being a Christian is that I'm not capable of living a sinless life. I remember talking to one of our youth interns at church after Gabriel's birth, and commenting on how "together" her life was. She seemed to be the "perfect" Christian. I couldn't imagine she fought against the same temptations I did. And maybe she didn't, but she looked at me and said, "Oh, Marnie, I may look like I have it all together, but I am so sinful." That's all she said. I was shocked. That's stayed with me all these years later, and I hang on to that. We are human, and we make mistakes. The goal is to turn from the sinful part of ourselves and try to do better. Some days are easier than others. Some days we fail miserably, but "the Lord is faithful. He will establish you and guard you against the evil one" (2 Thessalonians 3:3). Every day is a new day to get back on track. "The steadfast love of the LORD never ceases; his mercies never come to an end; they are new every morning; great is your faithfulness. 'The LORD is my portion,' says my soul, 'therefore I will hope in him.'" (Lamentations 3:22-24)

FINDING MY WAY

Moving back to my parents' house was a difficult transition. I was still at war with myself; fighting against my weaknesses, and trying to find where I belonged in this new family dynamic. I was a mother but also a daughter. I made my own rules but still followed the rules of my parents. We butted heads on more than one occasion; both sides trying to find the right balance, but we managed.

Living with my parents and working minimum wage at fast food restaurants allowed me to finally qualify for federal assistance. It was a lifted burden to know Jade's medical and physical needs would be met, and I knew it was only temporary. Applying for assistance was somewhat demeaning. Having a stranger go through your personal information and question your motives behind having to ask for help is humiliating. I was always asked where the father was and why I wasn't going after him for support. I tried to explain that it wasn't safe for me to contact him, but that wouldn't always work. Sometimes I told them I wasn't sure who the father was. I felt judged and ridiculed sitting in those government offices. There are those who abuse the system, but I didn't want to have to ask for help. At the time, I had no other choice. I also had to deal with the embarrassment of using food stamps; the looks and whispers from cashiers and other customers were awful. But I did it for Jade. The blessing in the whole situation was that I was able to take my daughter to the pediatrician I had visited when I was growing up. He was a member of our church and, as a favor to our family, took Jade on as a patient. I would take her to the free clinic for shots and well-baby checks, but if there was something wrong, I could go to our personal physician and he would see her. It was a great relief to me; I trusted him completely. In fact, he saved my daughter's life before she was a year old.

Jade got very sick one evening. By morning, she was so dehydrated that I could count the ribs on her tiny body. I called the doctor and he told me to bring her in. He ran some tests and said he was also going to run tests to rule out things he knew it couldn't be and started her on antibiotics. We went home, started her medication, and waited to hear from the doctor. When he called a few hours later, he told me to bring Jade back in quickly. The one thing he thought she couldn't have was the test that came back positive. She was suffering from a serious infection called shigella (a form of dysentery), which she'd acquired at the small daycare I placed her in while I worked. The health department went in and shut them down. It was a scary situation, but I was so thankful for God's provision.

I had to come up with another plan for Jade's care while I earned a little money and waited for the new school semester to start. During those early months, My parents would go to work in the morning, and I would spend the day with Jade, taking care of the household chores for my parents. Around 3:30, Daddy would come home to take over baby duty while I worked the late shift at one fast food chain or another. When Mama got home after 5:00, Daddy would return to the church and finish his work for the day. My shift would end a little before midnight and I'd come home to sleep. My parents lived in a small, two-bedroom townhome, and for four years, I slept on the foldout couch in the living room. Jade had a room to herself so I wouldn't wake her in the night coming home late from work. Motherhood was a challenge and I was glad to have my parents help with the mountain of details.

Working late hours and living with my parents again was awkward. I was used to living alone and being accountable to no one. Now I had a newborn and parents who demanded my attention most of the time. We had to make some concessions and compromise. We decided I would keep my independence, but as a courtesy, would let my parents know where I was going, or at least when I would return. That was established late one night when I didn't return home directly from my late shift at work. When I got home, my father was waiting for me. I'd just gone to get something to eat with some of the people I worked with, not thinking that Daddy would get up to check on Jade and realize I wasn't home at my usual hour. Again, this was before cell phones, so he had a right to be angry and concerned. I should have understood, even though my daughter was sleeping, she still needed me to be home and on call if something happened. I was still taking some things for granted.

One thing I didn't take for granted was my job. At the time, fast food was the only employment I could get that would give me enough evening hours to have a decent paycheck. Everyone should have to work in food service once in their lives; it teaches you more than you could imagine. I learned teamwork, multitasking, and a lot of patience! In the years since, I've watched too many people yell at and complain about fast food restaurant service and food. If you've never worked behind the counter, you have no idea how difficult a job it can be. The registers are diabolically confusing, and if everyone isn't on their A-game the whole process falls apart. Customers can be the worst when it comes to difficult orders and obnoxious attitudes. Next time you're stuck in the drive-thru, or standing at the counter, remember that a smile and a kind word go further than a snide remark or angry attitude.

AN UNEXPECTED BLESSING

My church family embraced us with no questions and no judgment. Jade didn't have just one set of grandparents, she had a whole building full of Grandmas and Grandpas that loved her and doted on her. She and I were truly blessed by our church family.

One of the best things that happened was a friendship that Jade created for me through her birth and our return to my hometown. Remember the youth minister's daughter? The one I did not get along with because we despised each other? Her name was Samantha. She moved home around the same time I did, and one day her mother came to visit and brought her along. Samantha fell in love with Jade and was a huge help to me in those first years of Jade's life. She watched Jade and took care of her like she was her own child. We put our past behind us and allowed Jade to bridge the gap between us. Jade was completely attached to Samantha and was even pictured in her wedding photos. Over the next few years, Jade would spend many days and nights with her and her family. Sam and I have often laughed and talked about the change in our relationship over the years. We are thankful that God healed the wounds between us and gave us a lasting friendship. Though we don't get to talk often, when we do, we pick up where we left off as though the years haven't separated us. Our friendship is one of God's many miracles in my life.

In fact, when my daughter got married, she was adamant that Samantha and her husband be invited. She had a small ceremony with just the closest family and friends. I was so happy they could be a part of her special day and said as much when we hugged after several years apart. She laughed and said, "Of course I came...my practice baby is getting married!" What a gift she and her family have been to us!

;

Chapter 10 - Questions & Reflections:

When have you had to swallow your pride and do something you didn't think you'd have to do in order to survive? How did you react? Were you thankful or bitter about the situation? How do you feel about it now in hindsight?

Is there something you're going through now that puts you in this type of situation? How are you handling it? What can you be thankful for in your present circumstance?

Read 1 Thessalonians 5:16-18 and write it below.

Meditate on the words and commit them to memory, then repeat them daily to prepare your heart and mind for whatever may come.

CHAPTER 11

September sent me back to college. Jade was closing in on her first birthday and was back in daycare. It was difficult to leave her behind in the mornings, but I knew it was the only thing I could do. I had to go to school full-time to qualify for aid, and neither of my parents could afford to sacrifice their jobs. I took every loan and grant offered over the next three years and worked hard to improve my withering GPA. I didn't like having Jade in daycare, but I didn't have much choice. It's one of the hardest things I've ever had to do.

School was much easier for me after Jade was born, which was ironic, because I had less time to myself. But I was more focused and able to stick to my graduation plan. I decided to become an English teacher because it was one of the few classes I enjoyed in school. Teaching would allow me to have a secure job and a means to provide for my daughter. I also wanted an occupation that gave me the opportunity to spend the most time with Jade. Holidays and summer vacation made teaching a better option than any office job. I wanted to teach high school and finished my degree with a B average. I loved every minute of it, but some people questioned my ability. They knew my struggles in school and were surprised by my desire to teach. To be honest, I surprised myself. I didn't have to work hard in high school, but I didn't really enjoy it. It had been more of a social scene for me. My mother was probably the most shocked. She questioned my choice when I told her what I wanted to do with the rest of my life, but I wouldn't be dissuaded. I wanted to teach.

I believe true teachers are born to it. You can fake it and do a good enough job, or you can fail miserably and hate every day you go to work. But if it's in your DNA, if it's what you're called to do, if it's your passion, there is nothing better! I was born to teach. I loved every moment and never doubted my decision.

What I doubted was whether or not I was going to get a job. Back then there were no job fairs or help from the university to help you get started. I graduated and got my teacher certifications in secondary English and U. S. History. I filled out applications for schools all over my hometown and the surrounding areas. Then I waited. And waited. And no one called. I tried not to panic. It was still early in the summer, but I was beginning to wonder if I would even get an interview. I wanted to teach high school juniors. I felt like they were the perfect grade level. They weren't seniors who were ready to get out of school, and they weren't immature freshman or sophomores. And there was no way I was going to teach middle school. My certification allowed me to teach seventh through twelfth grade, but I was not going to teach junior high. It wasn't going to happen. Juniors. That's what I wanted. Lucky for me, God knew what I needed better than I did.

In Jeremiah 29:11-14, the LORD speaks to the captives in Babylon. " For I know the plans I have for you, declares the Lord, plans for welfare and not for evil, to give you a future and a hope. Then you will call upon me and come and pray to me, and I will hear you. You will seek me and find me, when you seek me with all your heart. I will be found by you, declares the Lord, and I will restore your fortunes and gather you from all the nations and all the places where I have driven you, declares the Lord, and I will bring you back to the place from which I sent you into exile." God was getting ready to lead me out of my captivity. I was being faithful. I was praying, and trying to do what I believed He wanted me to, but I had to be patient. Patience has never been my gift.

Toward the end of June or the beginning of July, I received a call from one of the small districts about forty miles from my hometown. The principal started the conversation with, "We have an eighth grade English position open and wondered if you would be interested in applying?" Without a single thought, a resounding "Yes" fell out of my mouth and rushed across the phone lines. The principal gave me a time for my interview and when the phone clicked in my ear, I thought, "What have I done?" I went to the interview a few days later, spoke with the principal, toured the school, and was offered the job on the spot. I was speechless. This wasn't what I thought I wanted, but I had a peace about it, sitting in that office. I said yes and went home to tell my family.

Teaching in that small town set my life on a course I could never have imagined.

An Unconventional Love

I loved teaching eighth grade! Isn't it funny how God can give you things you don't even know to ask for? I also loved living in a small town where football was King and most people knew each other. Jade and I lived in a small rent house just down the street from the middle school. Half the students walked down our street to get home every day and played football on the pavement outside our house. On Halloween nights, our house would get wrapped in toilet paper not once, but four different times, by different groups of kids. One group of students threw register tape instead of toilet paper. I had huge sheets of paper blowing from my trees for days.

In a small town, you have an opportunity to get involved at all different levels of the school and community. My first year, I became a member of the local chapter of the largest state educator organization. They loved new teachers and I was anxious to help out any way I could. Over the next few years I served as secretary and treasurer for the local unit and traveled to Austin twice a year for conventions and leadership academies. I relished those mini-vacations with adults. My parents would take care of Jade and I got a much needed break. Being a single mom, you look for those opportunities for adult conversation and a short escape. I loved every moment of motherhood, but needed time to grow in my profession and used the opportunities when they presented themselves.

My parents were still very active in Jade's rearing even though they lived forty miles away. In West Texas, where land is plentiful and towns are spread thin among the tumbleweeds and oil derricks, forty miles is a short drive. The year after I moved out of my parents' house, my daddy took a job in the Texas Panhandle. My short drive changed to three hours, but I was lucky to have reliable transportation. I wore a rut in the roads between our two houses over the next few years.

The summer before my third year of teaching, I went to a leadership camp with two of my closest friends; we were headed for a long weekend of training and fun. A few days before we left, I drove Jade to my parents' house and returned home. The plan was to travel with my coworkers via a short plane ride to Austin, then fly out of Austin to Amarillo at the end of the conference. I would spend the following week with my parents and Jade, before returning for another week of gifted training for the upcoming school year. Mama and Daddy were pulling grandparent duty for almost three weeks in a row and I was very grateful.

We flew to Austin, and when we got to the conference hotel, we began to network and move from one session to the next. My two girlfriends introduced me to a number of educators from all around the state. But then a man approached our little group and I seemed to disappear from their view. They were so enamored by this guy that they actually turned away from me and focused all their attention on him. I'd never seen him before; he was older, gregarious, and affectionate toward my friends. They spoke for several minutes and then he moved away to another group. We were never introduced.

I thought little of it at the time. Men were not on my radar. I'd spent the first four years of Jade's life looking for a man to complete our family. I tried to date a few "good guys" who had their own issues and couldn't give me what I wanted, and I'd defaulted once or twice to the "bad boys" I was so fond of. I'd been so desperate for so long, it was hard to move past that default emotional setting. After several failed relationships, I finally came to the realization that the only person I could depend on was God. He was the only one who could fill the hole in my heart. I had to get to a place where I loved myself before I could love someone else. Maybe God wanted me to be single for the rest of my life. I needed to focus on being the best mother I could be and let the future go.

;

I was content.

I had a beautiful daughter, a job I loved, and a community and church where I belonged. It was enough. I told God, if He wanted me to pay attention to any man in the future, He was going to have to hit me over the head with him. I was done looking.

So, the conference was in full swing. We were in training sessions and meeting people. I continued to witness this mystery man on the fringes of my personal network. Then the night of the awards banquet arrived. We all dressed in our finest and had a lovely dinner while awards were given to outstanding educators and local groups. At the end of the dinner, there was a live band and dancing. I'm not much of a dancer. We didn't dance in my house growing up and I didn't really know how to dance with a partner, but everyone was having fun and getting out on the dance floor -- especially the mystery man. I'm not exaggerating when I say this: he danced with every woman in the room – even the woman who was wheelchair bound. But he did not dance with me. He wouldn't come near me. He worked his way through all my friends at our table, but avoided me like I had the plague. I started to wonder what was wrong with me.

The party ran late into the evening, but I left early and retired to my room. My brother was back in Austin, living with his wife and their new baby. He came by the hotel to visit me while I packed my bags to return home. The next morning, my girlfriends and I left for the airport. They had an earlier flight home, so I saw them off and waited to pick up my boarding pass for the flight to Amarillo that would have a short layover in Dallas. As I took my boarding pass and turned to find a seat in the waiting area, I saw the mystery man standing in the line behind me. We had never spoken, so I don't know what came over me, but I winked at him as I walked by. In my defense, it's what we do in our family. We wink. My daddy has winked at me since birth. It's a way to say "hey" I guess. At least, that's the way I meant it.

When he got his boarding pass, he and his two friends came to wait in the same area where I was and he struck up a conversation with me about the weekend and the conference. He asked where my friends were and I explained that I wasn't going back home yet, but had to travel to

Amarillo. When they called for us to board, he told his friends that he was going to sit with me on the plane since I was by myself. We actually all sat together at the front of the plane. This was when Southwest Airlines had the backward facing seats on the front row. I sat with my back to the cockpit and the mystery man sat facing me.

His name was Rod. He was an assistant principal and was traveling with two other principals from his district. We talked about a variety of things on that 40-minute plane trip. I told him I was interested in possibly moving to the Metroplex to teach; that living in West Texas was great, but I wanted more opportunities for my daughter to experience culture and art. He gave his business card to me with the names of the personnel director in his district and the phone number I needed to contact them for an application. During our conversation I told him I was traveling to visit my parents and see my daughter; mentioning the difficulty of being a single mother and trying to expose my child to all the things I wanted her to know and learn.

He asked for his business card back.

When he gave it to me the second time, it had every number available to reach him: home, cell, pager, and office. I jokingly responded, "So I can call you anytime?" Looking me straight in the eye, he said, "Yes. Anytime." Rod would tell me later that during our first conversation he was glad he hadn't flirted with me the evening before or while we talked because when he found out I had a daughter, he assumed I was married. When he'd seen me during the conference, he had thought I was too young for him and didn't want to be "an old fool" by striking up a conversation with me. When I winked at him in the airport, he thought, "Well, great. Now I have to talk to her."

When we got off the plane in Dallas, I had an hour layover until my next flight. Rod told his friends to go on ahead, that he would catch up with them later, but he would stay with me until my flight departed. I thought it was sweet of him to keep me company, but to be honest, he made me nervous. I had just met him, but I was attracted to his personality and confidence. I thought he was about ten years older than me, maybe around forty years old, but during our conversation on the plane, I'd found out his real age.

;

As a reference to something we were discussing, Rod had said, "When I graduated high school in 1969..." and I started laughing.

"What's so funny?" he asked.

"I was born in '69!" I said smiling.

"That's not funny," Rod replied.

I thought it was hysterical. Here was this guy, eighteen years older than me, but such a neat person to talk to and laugh with. I didn't know what to do with myself. I bought Jade a souvenir from the airport gift shop, and we stood at the gate waiting for my flight to be announced. When my flight was called, Rod put both hands on my shoulders and said, "I promise this won't take long." And he kissed me. Right on the mouth. I boarded the plane in a daze. I sat by the window and as the plane rose into the air, I thought, "What just happened?"

In Amarillo, as I disembarked from the plane, I saw my family in the distance and an announcement came over the PA system, asking me to report to the nearest Southwest Airlines' desk. My parents looked at me strangely as I shrugged my shoulders. Approaching the desk, I gave my name and one of the Southwest Airlines workers said, "Yes, a gentleman has asked that you call him as soon as you get to your parents' house," handing a note to me with Rod's name and phone number on it. Then the twenty questions from my parents started: Who was this guy? Why did he want me to call him? Where did I meet him? It was hard to explain to the preacher and my mother that I had just met the man who desperately wanted to speak with me and knew little about him.

Needless to say, when I arrived at my parents' house and got Jade settled down from seeing me and catching up on her "Momma" needs, I called Rod. He had been waiting by the phone. I think we talked for four hours that first night. And for some reason, we laid out all our dirty laundry; we talked about our entire histories. I shared the stories of Gabriel and Jade, Austin, home, and work. He spoke to me of his previous relationships, his children, his family, friends, and work. We knew all the dirty little secrets people sometimes never tell each other. Why we opened our hearts in that one moment, I may never understand. But that night and every night for the rest of the week we bared our souls to each other.

;

It was the end of July and Rod was already back at work from summer vacation. We met on a Sunday, and on Thursday I called his office, but his secretary answered. She said he was out in the building and unable to come to the phone, asking if she could take a message. When I told her who I was and that he could just call me when he returned to the office, she said, "Could you please hold? We've been instructed to find him if you call." I didn't know what to say to that. After a few moments of silence, Rod came on the line out-of-breath and opened our conversation with "Hey, I love you, how are you doing?" I froze. What did he just say? Did he just say he loved me? Is he crazy? My response was, "I appreciate the sentiment, but you realize I can't say that back to you." He said the sweetest thing. "I know, but it's how I feel. And I'm too old to play games. If you feel the same way, that's great, but if you don't, that's okay, too. I just can't waste time and not tell you how I feel." It's the best gift any man ever gave me. Love, with no strings attached.

I had no idea what to do with it.

The week ended and I headed back home for district training, leaving Jade with her grandparents for one more week. I continued to talk to Rod daily and when I returned the following weekend to pick up my daughter, Rod had sent two plane tickets for us to travel to see him. He wanted me to meet his friends, see where he lived and worked, and he wanted to meet Jade. We'd discussed this "thing" we had between us and he knew I was a package deal. I told him, in no uncertain terms, that Jade was the most important thing and if this didn't work out for her, it didn't work out for me. I nervously told my parents about the tickets. Expecting a lecture, I was surprised by a totally different response from my mother, "Do we need to start planning a wedding for next summer?" WHOA! Where did that come from? Who was this woman? I explained that I liked the man I spoke to on the phone, was maybe even falling in love with him, but I didn't really know him yet. I had no idea if we had any chemistry or if Jade would like him. It was very scary.

The following week, Jade and I packed our bags and traveled to the Metroplex. I was nervous to see Rod. We'd only met two weeks earlier, and most of our time together had been spent over long distance telephone lines. As the plane landed, I gathered our belongings and began the long walk up the connecting bridge from the plane to the gate. Jade knew where we were going and why. She knew she was going to meet the man at the end of the phone that she had talked to over the last few days. Clasping my hand, she kept looking around the legs of the adults in front of her and asking where Rod was. When I saw him standing just beyond the rest of the crowd at the gate, I bent down to Jade and pointed to him. "There he is," I said. Jade's chubby hand pulled from mine as she ran toward the man I was falling for. My heart leapt as he scooped her up into his arms. He shifted her to his hip, moved his other arm around me as I approached, and I knew I was home.

We spent the next several days with Rod, in his hometown, visiting his house, his work, and meeting his friends. He reserved a room for us at the closest hotel to his house and he spent time swimming with Jade and showing her around his high school. Jade was totally taken with him. He brought her a school jersey to sleep in and one of my favorite pictures is from the first night we were all together, the two of them in matching football jerseys, looking at a picture book together on the couch in the hotel room, her hair wet from her bath.

Eighteen days after we met, the night of freshman orientation at the high school where he worked, Rod pulled me into his office and proposed. I said yes, and he slipped an emerald solitaire on my finger. After the night's activities were complete, we returned to the hotel where I called my parents. Their response was calmer than I expected. My daddy only asked, "When do we get to meet him?" My mother's reply, "It took you guys longer than your daddy and me. We knew after ten days." The next call was to my brother. When he answered the phone, I said, "Hey, I just wanted to call you and tell you I'm getting married." He gasped loudly and responded, "You're not dating anybody!" Through nervous laughter I told him some of what had transpired over the last few weeks. He asked to speak to Rod on the phone. They spoke for a few moments and then my brother came back to me with surprise and guarded happiness, still not able to completely grasp what had happened in the eighteen days since I had seen him in Austin.

;

That was our whirlwind romance. We set the date for the following Memorial Day and all my friends back home thought I was crazy. One, for getting engaged so quickly and then for waiting until the school year ended to get married. They assumed that since we moved through the "dating" part so quickly, we would marry quickly, too. Most of them expected me to leave during the Christmas break and not come back. That wasn't what I wanted. I had made a commitment to my school and I intended to keep it. I knew if it was meant to be, we would be able to wait until the end of May to marry. We spent the next nine months traveling between our two towns, six and a half hours apart, to see each other. Every weekend Jade and I traveled to Rod or he traveled to us. We put a lot of miles on our vehicles, but needed the time to get to know each other and make sure this is what we wanted. Because we were always traveling on weekends, we rarely went to church, but I was convinced that even though we were raised in different denominations growing up, we would be able to find a place to worship when we got married. I was not in constant prayer about this, but I believed God had brought us together and would work it all out after the "I dos".

Though I was trying to do things the "right" way during those nine months before we got married, I'll be honest that I still had my demons to deal with. As a couple, we were not seeking God in our relationship. I thought I could be strong enough for both of us. But it doesn't work that way. In fact, once I thought God had answered my prayers about finding the right man to marry, I stopped communicating with Him daily and started relying on myself again.

;

Chapter 11 - Questions & Reflections:

Think about what you do for a living. It doesn't really matter what your job is (whether you work outside the home, work from home, own your own business, or are at work raising your children)...do you feel called by God to the work? Why or why not?

If you don't feel called to what you are doing, spend some time alone with God seeking His voice. Maybe He wants you to make a change, or maybe He wants to see a change in your attitude toward the job you're in right now until He's ready to move You. Ask Him for clarity and purpose.

Explain a time in your life when you thought you had a handle on everything and didn't need God. How did that work out for you? What happened when you stopped relying on Him and His will for your life?

Are you hiding from God right now? Are you unwilling to allow Him to control the narrative of your story at this moment? Ask God to forgive you for your rebellion and put your trust in Him alone.

CHAPTER 12

MARRIAGE IS HARD

After we got married, I realized that we hadn't been totally honest with each other. Rod had some issues, as did I, but I thought I could change him. This is one of the biggest lies women tell themselves. We believe if we love enough, or nag enough, we will change the way our men are wired. It's just not going to happen. My husband likes to say, "Women marry hoping to change men, men marry hoping women will never change." What I learned very quickly was that what love had blinded me to in the first nine months of our relationship, slapped me wide awake after we married. Rod and I didn't come from the same place. Not only did our age difference set us vastly apart, but our upbringings, our political views, and our faith all fell on different sides of a dividing line.

The first two years of our marriage were very difficult for me. The man I married was sometimes very different from the man I had spent all those hours traveling to see during the early months of our relationship. Rod could be sweet, giving, attentive and loving, but he could also be verbally abusive, angry, loud, without affection, and emotionally distant. Several times in the first year of our life together as a family, he would get angry at something we were discussing, raise his voice at me, slam doors, drive away in anger or threaten to move out of the house. Jade would run to her room crying and I would walk the backyard, tears streaming down my face, crying out to God asking what I had gotten myself into. Our biggest fights came on Sundays when I pestered him to come to church with us. He not only refused to come,

;

but many times belittled my faith. This was so different from what I thought marriage was supposed to be. Marriage takes work, even in the best circumstances, and I was unprepared for the battle that lay ahead.

I told no one about our life. To people on the outside we were a happy family. But sometimes the hard days outnumbered the good days, and I knew I had to do something. Somehow, I came across a book entitled The Power of a Praying Wife by Stormie Omartian.[6] It's not an exaggeration when I say this book saved my marriage. Reading the book helped me put my faith in the power of prayer and it changed me. The book is a month-long, daily devotional and prayer time for a wife to focus on her husband. Omartian asks you to pray for thirty days and see if you don't notice a difference in your life. Each day focuses on a specific area of a husband's life; things important to him as a man and as a provider, the way God made him. The most eye-opening moment for me was realizing I wasn't crazy. Men and women see things differently. We react to issues in different ways and understand things differently. It was liberating. Omartian's book gave answers to questions I didn't even know I had until I read the chapter and prayed the prayer. Interestingly enough, the hardest chapter to read through was the first one. That chapter dealt with me as a wife, and how women handle situations with our husbands. It challenged me to be open to God changing me instead of Rod. It was a bitter pill to swallow, but how wonderful the results!

Through prayer, I found that God wouldn't take away our problems, but He gave me the ability to react differently and find ways to cope with Rod's anger. He gave me wisdom and strength to stand up for myself and for Jade, and not let Satan have power over me and my emotions. One day after I had started praying through the book, Rod and I got into an argument that turned venomous. As he grew angrier about our discussion, he threw out the words that once brought me so much pain. Instead of crying or screaming at him, I responded with calm reason and refused to engage in the argument. With eyes open wide in stunned silence, he turned and walked away; the argument was over. God gave

6 Omartian, Stormie, The Power of a Praying Wife, Eugene, OR: Harvest House, 1997.

me peace to deal with our situation and hope for the future. I didn't look too far ahead, but tried to live one-day-at-a-time.

LIES WE TELL OURSELVES

Life can be an ugly cycle of failure, if you let it. As humans, we are weak and revert to old habits that are easier than what we know to be true. Society wants us to seek the easy pathway to change. Take this pill, use this cream, join this club, wear these clothes: you will be thinner, younger, happier, healthier, and more beautiful. If it were that easy, we'd all live perfect lives. But we are all born with a weakness inside us. Not everyone is tempted by the same sin. However, everyone is tempted by something. All sin is equal. It is our weakness that keeps us from perfection, and only Christ can make us perfect through His blood. But each of us has our own thorn in the flesh and our own cross to bear. Lying, cheating, pride, selfishness, bitterness, (the list goes on), are all sins that affect our hearts and minds and make us unworthy of the saving grace of Jesus. Thankfully, God loves us anyway, in spite of ourselves. Without Jesus, we cannot change our habits completely, but through Jesus we can do all things (Philippians 4:13).

Satan is the great deceiver. Just like when he approached Eve in the Garden of Eden, the devil comes to us with words we want to hear, and changes our focus from God to ourselves. I wanted so desperately to be married, to find a father for Jade, that I overlooked some of the things in our relationship that might have kept me from marrying Rod. I was blinded by love, by deception, by my desire to have a family. I didn't look too closely at what I had so as not to burst the bubble it was so tenuously wrapped in. In 2 Corinthians, Paul issues a warning about being "unequally yoked" with unbelievers. Many people use this as a reason not to associate with people outside their faith. However, Jesus spent a good portion of his time on earth with sinners, but his closest friends were followers of God. "Do not be unequally yoked with unbelievers. For what partnership has righteousness with lawlessness? And what fellowship has light with darkness?" (2 Corinthians 6:14). This passage is not talking about acquaintances and simple interactions. It is talking about walking in a united direction with someone who is spiritually on a different path from you. That's where the problems begin. I realized, after our marriage, that Rod and I were unequally yoked. Were there signs before we said our vows? Yes, but I didn't want to see them. Should I walk away from the commitment I made to be his wife? I didn't think so. "To the rest I say ([Paul], not the Lord) that if any brother has a wife who is an unbeliever, and she consents to live with him, he should not divorce her. If any woman has a husband who is an unbeliever, and he consents to live with her, she should not divorce him. For the unbelieving husband is made holy because of his wife, and the unbelieving wife is made holy because of her husband. Otherwise your children would be unclean, but as it is, they are holy. But if the unbelieving partner separates, let it be so. In such cases the brother or sister is not enslaved. God has called you to peace. For how do you know, wife, whether you will save your husband? Or how do you know, husband, whether you will save your wife?" (1 Corinthians 7:12-16).

No one should stay in an abusive relationship. I don't believe God wants that for anyone. My situation wasn't going to break me, unless I allowed it. Our marriage was hard. I think it always is, regardless of your situation. Living with another human being takes sacrifice. It's not easy, but I learned how to adapt to this new life. I taught Jade how to handle the hurtful things that came out of Rod's mouth in anger. I had to stand up to my parents and friends who wanted to be helpful, but sometimes made things worse. I knew I couldn't change Rod -- only God could do that -- but I also knew that maybe God wanted me to change. Maybe He wanted me to let go of some of the "perfect family" ideals I had in my heart and realize the only perfection I could seek was from God.

One of the hardest lessons learned was that maybe I needed to change as much as Rod did. That I needed to pray for my husband in specific ways so that I turned the focus from me to him, and from what I wanted to what God wanted to do in me. I did not want to become another statistic. I didn't want to add divorce to my laundry list of failures. Again, I'm not saying that staying with someone is the only answer -- just like adoption isn't for everyone, or raising a child alone is not the road others may choose. All I know is that in this instance in my life, God used Rod and our flawed marriage as a means to shape and mold me into a stronger woman, a better wife, and an empowered mother. I learned that I couldn't change my husband, but only my reactions to his anger. I learned to recognize the signs of his frustrations, his fears and doubts, and how they garnished his responses to our arguments on a regular basis. I listened to his speech, watched his reactions and realized the loneliness and abandonment he felt due to his lack of a relationship with God.

What I realized was I also allowed Rod to dictate my relationship with God. He would quote scripture and take things out of context to manipulate them into what he wanted it to be, or use the Bible to punish me and the things I believed. I learned how to stand up for myself and for my daughter so she could have a relationship with God and know there was a better way. "Who shall separate us from the love of Christ? Shall tribulation, or distress, or persecution, or famine, or nakedness, or danger, or sword? As it is written, "For your sake we are being killed all the day long; we are regarded as sheep to be slaughtered." No, in all these things we are more than conquerors through him who loved us. For I am sure that neither death nor life, nor angels nor rulers, nor things present nor things to come, nor powers, nor height nor depth, nor anything else in all creation, will be able to separate us from the love of God in Christ Jesus our Lord" (Romans 8:35-39). No one could change my relationship with God unless I allowed it. And only I could hide the light of Jesus in myself.

We are called to be examples for others. "You are the light of the world. A city set on a hill cannot be hidden. Nor do people light a lamp and put it under a basket, but on a stand, and it gives light to all in the house. In the same way, let your light shine before others, so that they may see your good works and give glory to your Father who is in heaven" (Matthew 5:14-16). It was my responsibility to be the light for my husband; to show him the way out of his internal struggle with darkness.

Choosing to let God control my life, I went to church faithfully and took Jade. One of the most profound moments I had was one Sunday, when our pastor made this statement during his sermon: "Wives, you are not responsible for getting your husbands to church." What? That can't be right? I'm supposed to nag him into submission, right? Then he said, "As adults, we are responsible for ourselves. You can't make someone come to church, and if you continue to nag and prod, it will only make things worse. You come and bring your children. God will take care of your husband." That very moment, I resolved to stop arguing with Rod about coming to church. It wasn't easy, but I made a conscious effort when I talked to him. Instead of, "Are you coming to church with us?" and starting an argument, I would say, "Jade and I are headed to church. We'll be home for lunch." There was no judgment, no condemnation, no expectation. And here's the interesting part: Rod would go with us occasionally. We had a small amount of peace. I made friends at church, read my Bible daily, prayed through my devotional books, and my relationship with God was stronger than it had ever been before. I had a purpose.

WAR ON MY FAMILY

Two and a half years into our marriage, the unthinkable happened: September 11, 2001. My husband had spent thirty years in the United States Coast Guard when I met him. Most of that time had been in the Reserves, but he had enlisted during the Vietnam War and volunteered and served in Desert Shield/Desert Storm, in Saudi Arabia. I had joked when we got married that he couldn't volunteer for any more wars because he was too old. He agreed.

That evening, as we huddled around the television, listened to the news commentary, and watched the Twin Towers fall again and again, Rod looked at me and said, "I'm not going to volunteer, but if they call me..." I responded, "You have to go." Two days later, he received the call, packed his bags, and reported for duty. Just like that, our lives were changed, like so many others across our nation.

Over the next two years, while my husband was called back to active duty on two separate occasions, the devil attempted to break my spirit. Satan didn't just attack me; he attacked my whole family and used any means necessary to do so. No area of my life was spared in the battle.

;

The only way to handle the overwhelming situations was to turn to God and cry out for help. I was in constant battle with Satan. When you are on the path to God, Satan wants to distract you any way he can, and God allows it for the purpose of glorifying Him and His sovereignty. One of our Bible class members once said, "If you're not running into the devil, you're running in the same direction he is." We should all be running away from Satan, but he will try to get in our way and turn us from the path God has for us. Even Peter, one of Jesus' closest friends, ran headlong into the devil's trap. Peter would deny Christ three times before the rooster crowed (Luke 22:54-62), but he would be restored in his faith and lead many to believe in Jesus. What Satan wanted to use for evil, God turned around for good. Peter had "a living hope through the resurrection of Jesus Christ from the dead" (1 Peter 1:3). I found that hope as well.

The first attacks during this time were physical and emotional. I was hospitalized and had to have a kidney removed. My father resigned his job right before the surgery and my parents moved into our tiny house to take care of me while Rod was away. While my father looked for another position, this placed a strain on our resources, living in such a small space and trying to make room for three generations again was taxing. When Rod returned from active duty the first time, living with my parents became a bigger strain, not only physically, but on our marriage as well. My parents and Rod were often at odds with each other over a variety of issues, and I was usually caught in the middle.

My mother-in-law's health was also in a steady decline. She was suffering from Alzheimer's, and I was in charge of her care during the periods when Rod was away. Dealing with doctors, nursing home staff, and government services was a daily struggle. Paperwork and financial issues related to her health were a constant problem. I found myself bitter and frustrated that I was the one having to care for her. It felt like everything in my life was in one big pile, holding me down.

But there was a bigger issue I was refusing to deal with.

I was hiding the fact that I was $50,000 in debt.

;

Chapter 12 - Questions & Reflections:

In what ways is Satan trying to keep you from being a great witness for Christ?

Who or what is Satan most likely to use in warfare against you? If you're not sure, take some time to ask God to show you where you are blinded by your own weakness or unbelief.

When have you felt like you were being attacked physically, emotionally, or spiritually? How did you cope with the attack? What did you do to fight against the enemy? If you don't think you've ever been under attack, take some time right now to pray for God's provision and wisdom when the attack comes. Make no mistake, no one will escape the fiery arrows of the enemy without God's help.

CHAPTER 13

TWO MASTERS

Stubborn, bitter, angry, and deceitful are all words to describe my early years as a wife. Blaming Rod for our issues didn't make anything better, it just helped me turn a blind eye to my own sin. Satan used my blindness to steer me away from the path I wanted to walk, until God intervened and showed my divided loyalty.

"No one can serve two masters, for either he will hate the one and love the other, or he will be devoted to the one and despise the other. You cannot serve God and money" (Matthew 6:24). I never thought this scripture applied to me because I never had any money. But I realized that "the love of money is a root of all kinds of evils. It is through this craving that some have wandered away from the faith and pierced themselves with many pangs." (1 Timothy 6:10). My sorrows were in direct relation to my insecurities about money and my blinded desire to spend whatever I could when I had money available. Retail therapy? Yes, please! If that meant charging up credit cards and getting more, that's what I did. I deserved it, or so I rationalized. My debt was still in control of my life and I had not told Rod how bad it was. To be honest, I was shocked when I finally sat down, in his absence, and totaled the amount of money I owed. Each month I simply paid the minimum due and didn't look at the balances. I didn't want to know. Living in denial didn't make it go away, it made it worse, and I was terrified to lay it out to Rod and explain what I had done.

When Rod returned from active duty permanently, I handed a letter to him one night and asked him to read it but not talk to me about it. I

;

was embarrassed, ashamed, and broken over this sin. God must have had a hand on him as he read it. He didn't get angry or yell at me, he simply asked how he could help. We researched the best way for me to get out of debt. I contacted a Christian debt relief counselor who set up payments and made arrangements with my creditors for repayment, and Rod took over all the household bills so I could use my money exclusively for my debt resolution. Five years of constant vigilance, God's grace, Rod's help, and I was able to be debt-free.

It hasn't always been easy, but I've done things over the years to help. The first was deciding to tithe to my local church. God tells us in Malachi 3:10, "Bring the full tithe into the storehouse, that there may be food in my house. And thereby put me to the test, says the LORD of hosts, if I will not open the windows of heaven for you and pour down for you a blessing until there is no more need." God's math doesn't necessarily make sense, but I always have money at the end of the month and when I've ever needed extra, the money shows up from the most unexpected places.

CHANGE IS COMING

Interestingly enough, while Rod had been away from us, God was working in his life as well. While on active duty, his roommate was a Christian and he held Rod to task about our relationship. I had my Bible class members praying for him the entire time he was gone, and when he returned from active duty, he not only went to church, but also began to attend Bible class with me. He started making friends. Rod had always talked about the hypocrisy of the church -- how it failed him in years past -- but our class was made up of "misfits" from all walks of life. We had members who were divorced, recovering alcoholics and drug addicts, weak, strong, old, and young, but we were committed to Jesus and to each other. It was a place he felt like he fit in.

It worked for a few years. We went to church as a family, but Rod was never "all in". He was like an egg, fragile and vulnerable, just waiting for a predator to come along and smash him into pieces. I tried to live in the moment and thanked God for the change; I thought it was enough.

;

Then we moved.

We had been living in my mother-in-law's house. I tried not to feel bitter about it and be thankful that we didn't have a mortgage, but it never felt like it belonged to us. We had her furniture, her pictures, and her dishes. Lots of the things we'd received as wedding gifts stayed in boxes and stored because there was nowhere to put it. The house was old and needed repair, but Rod couldn't find the time, or let go of the money to really get things fixed. This was one of the strongholds the devil had over him. We had money but he wouldn't spend it. He also couldn't make decisions about some things that needed to be done. He was so focused on the negative, he couldn't see his way to clarity. I saw the "glass half full," while my husband viewed the "glass half empty." We constantly butted heads over little things I just thought shouldn't be a big deal but were monumental to him.

Then one day out of the blue, he wanted to look at houses. We'd talked about it, viewed model homes over the years, made "dream" plans, but I never believed we'd actually do anything because he always came back to "fixing up the old house." We looked at homes in the next town over from us on a long weekend in January, and by Spring Break in March, we had moved into our new home. I thought the new house, new town, and new church would answer all my fears and frustrations and fill the emptiness I continued to struggle with. I was still searching for answers away from God, and though I was better than I had been in years past, I still wanted to rely on myself.

When we moved to our new home, Jade and I started going to the local church just across the street from our subdivision. I wanted Jade to make friends and believed we should get involved in our new community. I enjoyed the sermons and met some people, but didn't get connected like I wanted to. As before, I let life get in the way and made the choice not to be consistent with my church attendance. My excuses were plentiful and weak -- no friends, Jade was unhappy, too busy, Sunday was my only day to sleep in, etc.. My commitment to God was just as fragile as Rod's, and he wasn't interested in going to a new church, so the struggle continued.

;

Uphill Climb

The year before our move was one of the most difficult years of my professional career. Against my better judgment, and without really seeking God's guidance, I had agreed to help out our local teacher organization by running for office. I can admit now that pride was the ruling factor in my decision. Through a number of incidents and resignations, I ended up becoming President of the organization before I was prepared. Again, my pride influenced my better judgment, and I sought the power and prestige that the organization held within our town. I was pulled in a dozen different directions and was overworked, stressed, and frustrated for most of the year. As I tried to effect changes within the organization, I was met with opposition and sometimes hateful attitudes. One member called me at my office and spewed her venom through the phone. She accused me of disrespecting her and her position. When I apologized and explained that it had not been my intention to hurt her, this fellow Christian replied, "I won't accept your apology. You can't make it right!" and hung up the phone.

I was dumbfounded.

Then I got angry.

I reveled in my piety; I had done nothing wrong. How dare she attack me! After the call I proceeded to avoid her at all costs, "to save myself" and give me peace. That didn't work out like I thought it would. God had a different plan.

Three years in the new house, and I made the conscious effort to start back to church. I asked around for a Bible class and was told to visit one in particular. I went into the room, sat down and began to fill out the visitor form when I heard the voice from the phone speak from behind me to another member of the class. The woman I had tried to avoid for a year was sitting in the same Bible class. I couldn't believe it. I almost ran from the room. I enjoyed the lesson but couldn't get past the presence of my "nemesis" sitting in the same room with me. When I met up with Jade to walk into the sanctuary for worship, there she was again! I steered Jade to another part of the worship center and then practically ran from the building after the final prayer.

Needless to say, I didn't return to that Bible class, but looked around for other options. I think that's always a good idea when you start at a new church. You shouldn't just pick the first class you go to without looking around, but you shouldn't look for another place strictly out of fear or anger either. A few weeks later, Jade and I officially joined the church. I knew it was important for us to have a place to belong and get involved with other believers. The following Wednesday night, I showed up for choir practice. I'd been in the choir at our previous church and enjoyed the outlet it gave me for praising God. Guess who walked in and sat on the front row of the alto section? I couldn't believe it. I remember thinking, "Really, Lord? Are you kidding me? Of all people, you've put this person in my face over and over! What are you trying to tell me?" I went home that night resolved to figure out what He wanted from me.

God wanted more than my shallow daily Bible reading and prayer time for my family and myself. He wanted a real relationship with me. He wanted my heart to change, and he wanted me to pray for someone I didn't even like. God wanted me to start living like I believed what I read in His Word, "Love your enemies and pray for those who persecute you" (Matthew 5:44). But I really didn't want to.

This was when I learned to "fake it 'til you make it." When I first started praying for this woman, I would say, "God, I don't like her. I can't be in the same room with her, but I know You want me to pray for her. So I'm asking You to change my heart so that I will want to pray for her. Change my perceptions and my emotions so I can love her like You love her and free me from the bondage of my anger and unforgiveness." I prayed this over and over. I would even silently pray when I saw her at church, or in a professional setting. It actually got to a point where I was able to return to that first Bible class and sit in the same room with her.

Change wasn't immediate, but slowly my heart began to soften toward her. She mostly ignored me in the beginning, and then began to at least greet me when we saw each other. I found that I had no feelings toward her for a time, I didn't hate her like I once had, but love wasn't an emotion I would have expressed for her either. However, I continued to pray for her and for my feelings toward her.

A TEST OF FAITH

At this time, I was no longer a classroom teacher, but had finished my master's degree and become a school librarian. I spent eight years in the classroom teaching eighth grade English and U.S. History, and then opened a new elementary school as their librarian. After five years, I moved into the largest high school library in the district. For the first time, I was working closely with another librarian. It was difficult to find my place and work cohesively with another adult in the same workspace. I was used to working with other educators, but not sharing my space with another adult. The first year was very trying. I spent much of the time asking questions and looking to fit in on a new campus with new co-workers. Also, working with high school students after working with elementary students was a huge transition. What made it more difficult was the difference in teaching styles and personalities that the other librarian and I shared. She had a "no-nonsense, step-by-step, this is the way it's always been done" approach while my approach was "fly by the seat of my pants, let's try something new, leap before you look." Needless to say, we butted heads repeatedly. But more times than not, we came to a consensus and were able to put aside our differences to get the job done. I loved my job at the high school. The second year was better than the first; I began to get my confidence back and felt I was where I was supposed to be.

Then the bottom fell out.

In February of that second year, I received a call from our Library Director, Lisa. When I answered the phone, she asked me to close my office door and sit down. She then proceeded to tell me that the district was going to announce various budget cuts in the Board meeting that evening and my job was one of three librarian positions that would no longer exist. She had just learned this information from personnel and wanted to call me immediately even though she was driving home from an out-of-town conference. She was miserable with the news.

My first question, "Do I still have a job?" Lisa assured me that I did, but didn't know what it would be. When I asked how they chose who would be moved from the school, since there were two positions, she explained that the district was using campus seniority. The last one to come to the campus would be the one to leave. There were three "second librarian" positions being eliminated, but luckily, three librarians were retiring at the end of the year. At that time, Lisa didn't know who would get which position, but we would be placed in one of those libraries for the coming year. I was thankful for that small miracle, but unsure of what the future held. There were three of us without jobs and the three openings were going to spread us across the student population: one elementary, one middle school, and one high school.

When I went home that afternoon, I walked into the living room where my daughter and husband were watching TV and said, "I need to talk to you guys about something." My husband jokingly responded with, "You got fired." Then he saw my face and realized I wasn't in a joking mood. When I laid out for them what had happened, they agreed to help me pray for God's guidance. I prayed for peace and for strength to take on whichever position He wanted me to have. My answer came at the end of May; I was going into the high school position.

At the new high school, the library was supposed to stay open all day, but I worked alone. One of the Assistant Principals assigned two teachers to give me a break during the day so I could eat lunch or run an errand if I needed to. One of the teachers was the same woman I had been praying for the last three years. God has a strange sense of humor. She became a huge help to me and allowed me to take the time I needed to recharge everyday. She was diligent, sweet, and we became friendly toward each other. I finally saw the plan God had in place for our relationship – if I hadn't been praying all that time, I would have been miserable. As it turns out, we get along fine now, even break bread together on occasion. I doubt she even remembers the phone call so many years ago, but it's a great reminder to me of the grace of Jesus and how we should extend it to others. In fact, I had the word grace tattooed on my dominant wrist in Greek (χάρις) to remind me of the grace I've been given in Christ Jesus. Every time I look at it, I'm reminded we could all use more of God's amazing grace.

Chapter 13 - Questions & Reflections:

What or who would you say are the two masters in your life? What is competing with your relationship with God?

Think of a time when someone really hurt you. How did you handle the situation? Did you allow God to determine your actions? Why or Why not?

When have you been given "bad news" only to see God working things out for good?

CHAPTER 14

MIRACLES HAPPEN

Miracles happen every day. Sometimes we are unaware of the small ones and other times we are overwhelmed by the awesome power of God. One of the most significant miracles in my married life came as the answer to a twelve-year prayer: my husband's salvation.

Our daughter went off to college, and for the first time in our lives, my husband and I were alone. Rod had retired a few years earlier. We enjoyed our new freedom and began to spend a great deal of time together. We had Saturday "all-day dates" and Rod began to attend church with me again. He always wanted to go to the early service so he could have the rest of the day to himself, and he still wasn't interested in Bible class, or making friends, but he was in church and I was happy to have him beside me. He rarely missed a Sunday after Jade went off to school. I had continued the Power of a Praying Wife prayers, month after month, for the last twelve years. One Sunday I woke with a fierce migraine. I suffered from them most of my adult life, but had been free from them for several years. This one came out of nowhere and as Rod got up for church, I told him I was too sick to go. He said okay, but thought he would go ahead without me. This was strange by itself, so when he returned later than usual that morning, I was shocked by what he said to me as he came into the house.

"The longest walk I've ever made was down the aisle this morning."

I almost fainted! Then he began to tell me about the sermon and how he felt God prodding him to take the next step. I'm convinced that God kept me home that day because He knew I would have been running down the aisle after my husband with hands raised shouting "Thank you, Jesus!" and making a spectacle of myself. He said when the preacher asked him why he decided to commit to Jesus, my husband's response was, "How can I expect my daughter to seek my counsel, if I'm not seeking the counsel of my Heavenly Father?" Pretty profound. And boy, did he mean it!

That day my husband's life was completely changed. Everyone could see it. It reminded me of Paul's "Road to Damascus" conversion (Acts 9). When God spoke to Paul, he immediately recognized the Lord, and turned from his previous path of Christian persecution. Rod was not the same man after that morning in church. He was on a different path. A path laid out before him by God. It happened in God's perfect timing, in His perfect way. I had no idea how badly our family was going to need him to be on God's side.

Just two months later, Rod and I were staging an intervention with our daughter at college. Between her bad choices and the friends she had made, she was headed down a path to destruction. My husband and I prayed the entire two hours it took us to drive to her university and when we confronted her with the things we knew to be true, my husband was the calmest I had ever seen him in all the years I had known him. Later that night, when we gave Jade the opportunity to "come clean" and lay everything out before us without judgment or condemnation, we had no idea how bad things had gotten. Through tears she told us, "God can't forgive me for what I've done." I looked at my husband and realized we had a much bigger issue than we had originally thought. We prayed as a family that night for the first time ever, brought our daughter home for the holidays, and used the next month to redirect and focus our lives with God as our centerpiece. It was a difficult time but one we cherish in hindsight. If God's timing hadn't been perfect, we might have lost our daughter to Satan's desires, but God is good, and restored our family.

OUT OF MY COMFORT ZONE

The New Year brought new challenges for us all, but that's the beauty of life. It is always changing and challenging us. My husband decided he

;

would go on three mission trips during the year; two stateside and one to the Czech Republic. He asked me if I'd like to go to Czech with him and I quickly said no. Missions weren't my thing; God didn't want me to be a missionary. But I would happily keep the home fires burning for his return.

For the next solid month, it seemed like every sermon I heard and every Bible class I attended had something to do with missions. Then at our women's retreat, the guest speaker spoke on foreign missions. The entire weekend, all I heard was a whisper in my head that said, "You're supposed to go to Czech." By the time I got home, I was sure I had lost my mind and through tears told my husband I thought I was supposed to go to Czech with him.

He was thrilled; I was terrified!

It was a life-changing experience. People say it all the time about missions, but it's true. I will never be the same. The trip was one of the hardest and most rewarding things I've ever done. My husband and I had our time in the valley. Before we were in the country 24 hours we owed money to a Czech man for our transportation into town. He graciously paid for our ticket when our methods of payment were insufficient. I also understand better how immigrants feel when they enter our country and don't speak English. There's nothing quite like being in a country where nothing is posted in your native language. Plzen, CZ is where I had my first (and only) full-on panic attack, but God surrounded me with people to get me through it. We also experienced the mountaintop in so many wonderful ways. The Czech Republic and its people are beautiful inside and out. When you are doing what God calls you to do, everything will be okay. And watching people come to know Jesus is amazing.

I've returned to Czech several times to visit friends I have made and to make new ones. My husband and I even toy with the idea of living there some portion of the year if we can manage it in the future. In fact, Rod taught English conversation and lived in Plzen for a year, working in the school where we'd done missions. It was a great experience for him, and one I'm so thankful he took. When you hear the call to go, answer it as Isaiah did, "Here I am! Send me." (Isaiah 6:8).

;

I used to think mission work was a suggestion, or for someone other than me, but God will continue to call until you answer, and it's always best to obey. His Great Commission is for everyone who follows Him. "Go therefore and make disciples of all nations, baptizing them in the name of the Father and of the Son and of the Holy Spirit, teaching them to observe all that I have commanded you. And behold, I am with you always, to the end of the age" (Matthew 28:19-20). Being obedient may not send you to a foreign land; it may only take you next door to your neighbor. But go where God sends you.

GOD IS GOOD

So many good things have happened in the years since Rod and I have been on our Jesus walk together. Our daughter, Jade, graduated from college and began working in the small town just 10 miles away from our home. She moved back in with us and spent two years paying off her loans and saving money for a place of her own. At the end of her first year, she showed me a library opening in her district and though I hadn't thought I would leave where I'd been working for 17 years until I retired, God had other plans for me.

I finished the last eight years of my educational career working with my daughter in a small district where I was able to do the job I'd always dreamed of but was unattainable at my previous district. I made new friends and enjoyed the pride and spirit that only a small rural district can know. I retired with 28 years as a teacher/librarian and was lucky to love my job until the very last day.

Strangely enough, two years before I retired, God gave me another avenue to explore. He introduced me to a direct-selling company that has given me an opportunity to love on and bless others, while building a sisterhood of support I never knew I wanted. I am so thankful for the women He's put in my path and the passion He's given me at this stage of life that fills me with purpose and achievement.

God also blessed Jade with a wonderful man who came into her life at the perfect time. Rod and I are so thankful that he loves Jesus first and that their marriage is built on a foundation of seeking God's will for their life together. I cannot wait to see what the Lord has in store for them!

Finally, one of the biggest blessings of our lives has been the restoration of Rod's relationship with his children from a previous marriage. We had been estranged from one of his daughters and her family for 17 years, but God built bridges and softened hearts, bringing us back together. We missed so many milestones and memories, but by the grace of God, we are forging new paths, healing old wounds, and finding joy in every new day we have as a family. I praise God for His goodness and mercy and His ability to perform miracles in every aspect of our lives.

THE FUTURE

Living the retired life, Rod and I enjoy our time together every day, trying not to take any of our blessings for granted. We love to say "every day is Saturday except Sunday" and I'm so thankful and content with the life we've built. We are both very involved in our local church, teaching classes, singing in choir, and finding whatever hole needs to be filled and trying to fill it with whatever ability God grants us.

God has taken a broken, sinful girl and turned her into a woman passionate to do His will. I follow Him without reservation. Do I still sin? Yes! "For all have sinned and fall short of the glory of God" (Romans 3:23). But just like Paul, I remember where I have been and where I am headed. "The saying is trustworthy and deserving of full acceptance, that Christ Jesus came into the world to save sinners, of whom I am the foremost" (1 Timothy 1:15), yet I will "run with endurance the race that is set before us, looking to Jesus, the founder and perfecter of our faith, who for the joy that was set before him endured the cross, despising the shame, and is seated at the right hand of the throne of God" (Hebrews 12:1b-2).

By the grace of God, I have changed my default setting from defense to offense. "Be sober, be vigilant; because your adversary the devil walks about like a roaring lion, seeking whom he may devour. Resist him, steadfast in the faith, knowing that the same sufferings are experienced by your brotherhood in the world. But may the God of all grace, who called us to His eternal glory by Christ Jesus, after you have suffered a while, perfect, establish, strengthen, and settle you. To Him be the glory and the dominion forever and ever. Amen" (1 Peter 5:8-11).

;

Chapter 14 - Questions & Reflections:

Have you ever been given an ultimatum or had to give one to someone you love? How did it play out?

What has God asked you to do that terrifies you? Are you doing it anyway? Why or why not?

List some of the blessings God has given you. Take time right now to thank Him for everything on your list.

PART 4; LESSONS LEARNED

"Take my yoke upon you, and learn from me,
for I am gentle and lowly in heart,
and you will find rest for your souls."

Matthew 11:29

"For whatever was written in former days
was written for our instruction,
that through endurance and through
the encouragement of the Scriptures
we might have hope."

Romans 15:4

CHAPTER 15

God has been so good to me but I couldn't always see Him working. Sometimes we lose sight of the path we should be on and allow the world to dictate how and why we live the way we do. Like the Israelites in the Old Testament, we forget the good things God has promised and the lessons He has taught us.

I want to be like Abraham, "No unbelief made him waver concerning the promise of God, but he grew strong in his faith as he gave glory to God, fully convinced that God was able to do what he had promised. That is why his faith was "counted to him as righteousness"" (Romans 4:20-22).

May we all learn from our mistakes and work hard to keep from repeating our past.

Follow God

Make a commitment to be a child of the King. He has given us the keys to the kingdom if we only trust in Him and take the gift of His Son's salvation. You will never be alone again. Understand that following God doesn't mean everything will be fine. There will be trials. In fact, trials are one thing we are assured of. "If they persecuted me, they will also persecute you. If they kept my word, they will also keep yours. But all these things they will do to you on account of my name, because they do not know him who sent me" (John 15:20-21). Regardless of what is in your future, God is always the best choice!

If you've never trusted in Jesus, let me share this with you:

;

God is holy, that means He's perfect. He's so perfect, corruption cannot live with Him. On the other hand, we have rebelled against God and this corrupted us. For example, we are selfish, we are prideful, and we lie. And this is our big problem: if God is perfect and corruption cannot live with Him, and we are corrupt...WE cannot live with God. Our corruption has cut us off from God, both now AND when we die, which means we must spend eternity in a lake of fire called Hell. But that is not what God wants. God loves you so much that He gave away His only Son to save you. Jesus Christ died on the cross in your place to pay the penalty for your corruption and rose again on the third day. Now, Jesus Christ will forgive you of your corruption, reconcile you with God, and give you the life God has always intended for you if you will:

1. Admit to Jesus Christ you are corrupt.
2. Believe He is the Son of God who died on the cross to save you.
3. Confess Jesus Christ as Lord (King) of your life.[7]

If you just confessed Jesus Christ as Lord of your life for the first time, I celebrate with you and pray you will take the next steps of finding a local church so you can grow and know Christ more fully. Welcome to the family!

PRAY

"Do not be anxious about anything, but in everything by prayer and supplication with thanksgiving let your requests be made known to God. And the peace of God, which surpasses all understanding, will guard your hearts and your minds in Christ Jesus" (Philippians 4:6-7). I cannot stress enough how important it is to be in constant prayer and communication to the one who created you. It's hard to hear God if you're not talking to Him and listening for His voice. "Rejoice always, pray without ceasing" (1 Thessalonians 5:16-17). He is the only one who can give you the answers you so desperately seek. God knows what we want and need, but He desperately wants us to ask Him for help.

---

[7] "Tools, Training & Apps | First Baptist Church Forney," n.d., https://fbcforney.org/tools/.

;

STUDY

Reading the Bible goes hand in hand with prayer. The only way we can learn what God wants from us is to be a student of His Word. The Bible is our textbook for life. It is a living, breathing, holy inspired means of open communication. "All scripture is breathed out by God and profitable for teaching, for reproof, for correction, and for training in righteousness, that the man of God may be complete, equipped for every good work" (2 Timothy 3:16-17). There is no time limit on good literature and the Bible is the best book on Earth. As we follow God and pray, we can't know His will or what to follow if we don't know the truth found in scripture. Too many of us are scripturally illiterate and allow our emotions or the beliefs of those around us to shape our actions. Read, study, and find what the Bible has to say for your life.

GIVE

Dave Ramsey, creator of Financial Peace University and other tools for money matters,[8] says you should save like no one else, so you can give like no one else. When I took the course, it helped me change my entire relationship with money. Giving is a personal thing between each person and God. "Each one must give as he has decided in his heart, not reluctantly or under compulsion, for God loves a cheerful giver" (2 Corinthians 9:7). But giving should be a part of your relationship with God. "Give, and it will be given to you. Good measure, pressed down, shaken together, running over, will be put into your lap. For with the measure you use it will be measured back to you" (Luke 6:38).

FELLOWSHIP

God did not create us to be an island, isolated from others, living on our own. He made us for fellowship and relationships. In the beginning, God said it wasn't good for man to be alone (Genesis 2:18). Jesus went to the synagogues, he spoke to groups large and small, but He had a close relationship with twelve men. He worshiped with them regularly. We

---

[8] Ramsey Solutions, "A Proven Plan for Financial Success | RamseySolutions.com," n.d., https://www.ramseysolutions.com/.

should spend time alone with God in prayer and personal study, but He also wants corporate worship. "And day by day, attending the temple together and breaking bread in their homes, they received their food with glad and generous hearts, praising God and having favor with all the people. And the Lord added to their number day by day those who were being saved" (Acts 2:46-47). God wants His followers to be part of a family, standing together for truth and bearing "one another's burdens" (Galatians 6:2).

SERVE

A former pastor of ours once told us, when it comes to serving the church, "find a hole and fill it." The church is supposed to work like the body – all parts working together for the benefit of the whole. If we all simply come to "sit and get" our weekly pep talk, we're not doing anything to advance the work of the church. Classes don't get taught, meals don't get delivered, music doesn't get performed, technology doesn't broadcast, prayers don't get lead, and members don't get cared for if we don't all pitch in to do our part. Make sure you're finding a place to serve in your local church to support the body of Christ. "For the ministry of this service is not only supplying the needs of the saints but is also overflowing in many thanksgivings to God" (2 Corinthians 9:12).

BE BOLD

To be honest, this is one I still struggle with, but God wants us to be bold in our faith. We aren't supposed to hide in a closet and keep the Good News to ourselves. "Since we have such a hope, we are very bold" (2 Corinthians 3:12) There are days I don't feel bold at all! But God wants us to share what we have with others. It's not easy, but it's simple. Everyone has a story; share yours. Jade likes to say, "People can argue with you about the Bible; they can't argue with you about your story." Step out in faith and show someone Jesus. You may be the only Bible anyone ever reads. "But the righteous are bold as a lion," (Proverbs 28:1b) so "be strong and courageous. Do not be frightened, and do not be dismayed, for the Lord your God is with you wherever you go" (Joshua 1:9).

BE THANKFUL

Find the positive aspects of your life and see the blessings God has provided for you. "Give thanks in all circumstances; for this is the will of God in Christ Jesus for you" (1 Thessalonians 5:18). It's so easy to get sucked into the overabundant lifestyle we live or to wallow in our sufferings that we forget to look for God's hand in our lives. Don't ignore His presence in your life. I used to think the cup was half full, but now I realize my cup overflows at all times. Find ways to express thanks for the life you have, no matter what it may be. My blessings are limitless and I can find thanks in any situation. "Oh, give thanks to the Lord, for he is good...This is the day that the Lord has made; let us rejoice and be glad in it...Oh, give thanks to the Lord, for he is good!" (Psalm 118:1, 24, 29).

LOVE

Christ died for us because He loved us. God tells us to love. Not just your neighbor, not just your family, not just those who love you back but everyone. "A new commandment I give to you, that you love one another; just as I have loved you, you also are to love one another" (John 13:34). We must love others more than we love ourselves. We have to love as Christ loves. "Let love be genuine" (Romans 12:9). "Little children, let us not love in word and talk, but in deed and in truth" (1 John 3:18) "Love does no wrong to a neighbor; therefore love is the fulfilling of the law" (Romans 13:10). "With all humility and gentleness, with patience, bearing with one another in love, eager to maintain the unity of the Spirit in the bond of peace" (Ephesians 4: 2-3). "So now faith, hope, and love abide, these three; but the greatest of these is love" (1 Corinthians 13:13). "Beloved, let us love one another, for love is from God, and whoever loves has been born of God and knows God. Anyone who does not love does not know God, because God is love" (1 John 4:7-8).

;

Brother Jimmy Pritchard used to say, "If I love God, and you love God, and we love each other, there is nothing Satan can do to us," "for He who is in you is greater than he who is in the world" (1 John 4:4).

———————————

There are days when I wish I could turn back time and change some of the things I did in my past, but then I realize that every one of those circumstances has molded me into the person God wants me to be. I would not give up a single mistake or moment of utter despair if it meant I would love God less or lack the relationship I have with the Father. My God is everything to me and I thank Him for the life I have. It belongs to Him.

"Thus says the Lord: "Keep your voice from weeping, and your eyes from tears, for there is a reward for your work, declares the Lord, and they shall come back from the land of the enemy. There is hope for your future, declares the Lord, and your children shall come back to their own country. I have heard Ephraim grieving, 'You have disciplined me, and I was disciplined, like an untrained calf; bring me back that I may be restored, for you are the Lord my God."

Jeremiah 31:16-18

Grace and Peace.

ONE MORE THING

Music has always been a big part of my life. I learned to sing acapella when I was a child and now my love of praise music knows no bounds! I've been lucky to perform in front of large and small crowds, and if I could sing for you, these are the songs that best fit my journey to loving Jesus without reservation and knowing God's love and provision for my life. Enjoy!

- *Amazing Grace* (Acapella) by Anthem Lights
- *Truth Be Told* by Matthew West
- *Redeemed* by Big Daddy Weave
- *Oh But God* by The Worship Initiative
- *Even If* by MercyMe
- *Known* by Tauren Wells
- *You've Already Won* - Radio Version by Shane & Shane
- *Graves Into Gardens* (Studio) by Elevation Worship
- *Take You At Your Word* (with Benjamin William Hastings) - Live by Cody Carnes
- *In Jesus Name* (God of Possible) by Katy Nichole

ACKNOWLEDGEMENTS

First, I want to thank God for the life He's given me. It's not been easy, and I've made things more difficult by the choices I've made, but He has NEVER left me. May the rest of my days glorify Him in all I say and do.

Second, I want to thank my family for standing by me and loving me in spite of myself. Their support is beyond measure, and God blessed me with exactly what I needed in the family He has given me.

Next, I want to thank Amianne, Eddy, and Leslie for reading the first draft of this book many years ago, Dee and Lisa for reading the revised manuscript when God told me to publish it, and Jade who made sure my grammar and details were correct. I am forever in your debt. I could not have done this without the support of great friends and those who believed I had a story to share.

Finally, I thank God for the teachers, preachers, and churches that have nurtured me my entire life. But I want to especially acknowledge these: Golf Course Road Church of Christ (Doug Parsons - pastor), Mimosa Lane Baptist Church (Rocky Pope - pastor), First Baptist Church Forney (Jimmy Pritchard and Nathan Lino - pastors). These men, and the congregations they shepherded, showed me the truth of God's Word and the love of God without reservation.

-- Marnie

Made in the USA
Monee, IL
13 February 2025

11976611R00085